cool
camping™

England

D1225355

Jonathan Knight

with additional contributions by Shellani Gupta and Andy Stothert

who should use this book?

If you live in a town or city, if you don't get enough fresh air, if you'd like to see more of the English countryside, if you like the idea of a quiet pint in a quaint country pub, if you can do without TV for a day or two, if you fancy trying something different, if you've had a tent in the loft since your aunt gave it to you for your 17th birthday, if you like the idea of camping but don't know where to go, if you've been camping before but you're totally over noisy sites next to main roads Thank You Very Much, if you're partial to a relaxing weekend away, if you're up for a walk or a surf or a bike ride or a bit of fishing, if you've always wanted to toast marshmallows on a campfire, if you're keen to try camping but are definitely not going if the weather turns nasty…

then this book is for you.

Because that's us too.

Enjoy!

The publishers assert their right to use
Cool Camping as a trademark of Punk Publishing Ltd.

The *Cool Camping* logo is under application
as a registered trademark with the Patent Office.

Cool Camping: England
First published in the United Kingdom in 2006 by
Punk Publishing Ltd
26 York Street
London
W1U 6PZ

www.punkpublishing.com

www.coolcamping.co.uk

Copyright © Jonathan Knight 2006

The right of Jonathan Knight to be identified as the author of this work has been asserted
in accordance with sections 77 and 78 of the Copyright, Designs and Patents Act 1988.

All rights reserved. No part of this publication may be reproduced, stored in a retrieval
system, or transmitted in any form or by any means, electronic, mechanical, photocopying,
recording or otherwise, without prior permission in writing from the publishers.

Any copy of this book, issued by the publisher as a paperback, is sold subject to the condition
that it shall not, by way of trade or otherwise, be lent, resold, hired out or otherwise
circulated, without the publisher's prior consent, in any form of binding or cover other than
that in which it is published and without a similar condition including these words being
imposed on the subsequent purchaser.

A catalogue record of this book is available from the British Library.
ISBN-10: 0-9552036-0-0
ISBN-13: 978-0-9552036-0-2

10 9 8 7 6 5 4 3 2 1

introduction

There are many books on the subject of camping, with hundreds, even thousands of campsites featured in each. So how do you find the truly exceptional sites? That's where *Cool Camping* comes in.

Camping has seen a surge in popularity in recent years and a complete change of profile. It's no longer the domain of retirees, towing their caravan slowly along the motorway to their regular plot in Whitstable. A different generation has taken over: young, professional urbanites in search of fresh countryside and adventure; festival campers who want to use their tents more than once a year; young families in which the parents value fun as much as the kids do.

This new generation of campers needs a particular book to guide them to the real treasures of England's countryside. And that book is *Cool Camping*.

In this first edition, we've compiled a selection of just 40 very special campsites, travelling the length and breadth of England to bring you our personal choice of favourite places to pitch your tent.

They're all designated campsites with the usual amenities – all have flush toilets and hot showers unless otherwise stated – but importantly, we don't judge the campsites exclusively on the quality of these facilities. We leave that to the other books. We're more interested in the location, the view, the surrounding area – even the philosophy and attitude of the staff and owners. We're looking at that almost immeasurable combination of factors that contributes to a site's overall character, helping to create a very special place to camp.

We might be swayed by a remote location, a stunning view or simply the fact that it's right next to a surf beach. There might be an opportunity to camp in a yurt, a tipi or a vintage trailer. We might recommend a delightful campsite in a hidden valley, even though the shower block has seen better days. But we'd never recommend a pristine site with fantastic facilities if it's next to a motorway.

One thing you can be sure of: we left all the featured campsites knowing that someday, we'd like to return. And what more of a recommendation could you want?

An incredible number of campsites have recently followed the 'holiday park' route, packing the grounds full of bulky, semi-permanent static caravans, installing a tacky clubhouse with a fast-food restaurant and bombarding the visitor with lists of rules and regulations. To us, that's not camping – that's holiday hell. It has also made our job of finding special, untouched sites, all the more difficult. But the 40 sites included here are testament to the fact that this journey has been worthwhile. More importantly, it means you can save yourself the effort of having to seek them out.

Aside from a few special entries that offer something completely different (see p16), the sites have been selected to appeal to the tent camper rather than the caravanner. That's not to say that caravans aren't accepted at these places – many do take caravans as well – but tenters' needs are slightly different and that has been our first concern when compiling this book.

Cool Camping is ideal for new campers, as it includes a good selection of well-organised sites with decent facilities. It also takes the guesswork out of picking a site, so there is more chance of your first camping trip being a memorable one for the right reasons. But experienced campers will also find this book useful, because they understand the difficulty in finding a really superb site. The only requirement for the user is that they should share our vision of what constitutes a good campsite.

In today's smaller, highly mobile world, the contemporary camper is just as likely to spend a weekend in a boutique hotel in Barcelona as to grab their tent and head for Cornwall. It's not a cost issue that has driven the resurgence of camping, but the need for something different; to break free from predictable packaged weekends and low-cost airline indifference. People are realising that a camping break in the wilds of Britain can be a far richer experience than a weekend in a swanky hotel. After all, today's hip hotel may be worn and tired next year, but the beauty of nature is lasting.

campsite locator

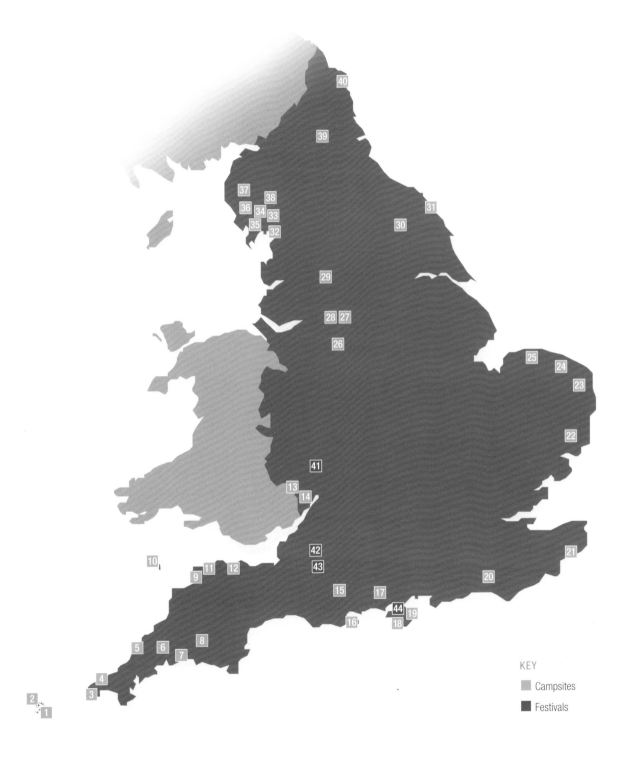

KEY

Campsites

Festivals

cool camping top 5

Our pick of the pitches; the five most memorable campsites in England, personally chosen by the Cool Camping team. Who says we can't count?

1 Blackberry Wood, Sussex

Reserve a forest clearing for two and order a campfire: the ultimate romantic camping break.

2 Troytown Farm, St Agnes, Isles of Scilly

Remote, water's-edge paradise with views to America (ish).

3 Wasdale Head, Lake District

Get high on mountains amongst the tallest peaks in the country.

4 Side Farm, Lake District

The most scenic campsite in all England? Just maybe.

5 Little Meadow, Devon

Cute, environmentally friendly and yes, the meadow may be little, but the Atlantic view is huge!

5 Vintage Vacations, Isle of Wight

Leave the tent behind and book one of these silver sixties trailers.

campsites at a glance

troytown farm, st agnes

If camping on the tiny island of St Agnes isn't exciting enough, it's certainly an adventure getting there. Take your pick from a boat, plane or helicopter ride for the journey to the Isles of Scilly's main islands, Tresco or St Mary's. The plane has the edge for maximum thrill, a tiny eight-seater bouncing about on the winds. Bag one of the front seats, inches from the whirring propellers, for a bird's-eye view of the 100-odd islands that make up this archipelago.

Then it's on to a catamaran for the trip to St Agnes. If it's a bright day, you'll be greeted by the almost Mediterranean sight of boats moored on the turquoise waters of Porth Conger as you arrive. Next is a tractor ride – for your luggage at least. Most people choose to let their bags go ahead and walk the 20 minutes to the campsite, a scenic stroll that provides a stunning introduction to the island.

At just one mile in diameter, St Agnes is one of the smallest inhabited islands of the Scilly archipelago. It's a beautiful, rugged place that has seen little change since Celtic times, a forgotten outpost of England's west. The majority of the island's 70 inhabitants work in flower farming during the winter months as they have done for generations, although tourism is now as important to the economy. Even so, there are only a handful of B&Bs on the island – most people come to stay at Troytown Farm, England's westernmost campsite.

Its position couldn't be any more remote or spectacular. The campsite clings to the western foreshore of the island, just feet away from the rock-calmed Atlantic waters that look as if they might engulf the campsite at high tide. To one side, a beautiful curve of sand at Periglis Beach extends into the sea. To the other, bold, intriguing rock formations add interest to the heather-covered coastal landscape. It's a magical wilderness that feels like the ends of the earth. In fact, it is almost at the ends of the earth; the nearest neighbours to the southwest are New Yorkers.

There are small, separate fieldlets with low hedges and walls offering a certain amount of protection from the elements, but this can be a windy island so come prepared. When the sun shines though, this place is perfect. You can play in the rock pools, spot the rare, migrating birds or just sling up a hammock and listen to the waves gently

lapping on the foreshore. At night, the lack of light pollution affords incredible views of the Milky Way and dazzling displays of shooting stars. Isolation is this island's greatest asset, so bring a love of nature and plenty of books to read.

The island may be remote, but it's fairly self-sufficient. Troytown Farm has a small dairy herd producing milk and cream for the island. They also rear pigs and grow vegetables to provide campers with food, so most survival essentials are available at the farmhouse.

The other of life's necessities is available by the pint at The Turks Head in Porth Conger,

the island's only pub. Perched on the hillside overlooking the bay and the adjacent islet of The Gugh, it might just win the prize for best beer garden view in England.

St Agnes is also blessed with some fantastic beaches. As well as Periglis Beach near the campsite, there's the small, sheltered beach at Cove Vean on the eastern shore and a sandbar at Porth Conger, where you can splash about in the waves or walk across to The Gugh at low tide. But for great sunset views, head back to Periglis – and see if you can't spot the Statue of Liberty in the distance.

THE UPSIDE: Extreme Atlantic isolation, one of England's most naturally beautiful campsites.

THE DOWNSIDE: Not easy to get to!

THE DAMAGE: It's complicated. Rates vary during the season from £5.75 to £7.25 per person. In peak season an additional charge of £1–£5 per tent applies. Luggage transportation £2.50 per person.

THE FACILITIES: Traditional-style granite building contains good facilities including flush toilets, hot showers (tokens required), coin-operated washing machines and dryers, shaver points, baby-changing facilities and hot drinks machine.

NEAREST DECENT PUB: The Turks Head, Porth Conger. The great food and beer is surpassed only by the view.

IF IT RAINS: If the weather gets really bad (and it has been known to be windy here!) Troytown Farm also offer self-catering accommodation in a chalet and cottage.

GETTING THERE: Contact Isles of Scilly Travel (0845 710 5555; www.ios-travel.co.uk) for plane and boat travel or British International (01736 363871; www.islesofscillyhelicopter.com) for helicopter services. Contact Troytown Farm for details of transportation to the campsite.

OPEN: Mar–Oct; winter by arrangement. Advance bookings essential during Jul & Aug.

IF IT'S FULL: Bryher Campsite (p22) is just a boat trip away.

Troytown Campsite, Troytown Farm, St Agnes, Isles of Scilly TR22 0PL | t | 01720 422360 | w | www.troytown.co.uk

bryher campsite

The tiny island of Bryher, Isles of Scilly, has two distinct faces. To the south and east, calm blue waters fill the narrow, sheltered channel between the island and its larger cousin, Tresco. Boats come and go unhindered while sunbathers enjoy the sandy beaches at Green Bay and the secluded cove of Rushy Bay. The northwestern shores, however, are a jagged jumble of weather-torn rocks, beaten and broken by the relentless Atlantic waves. Gales sometimes lash this coast with thousand-ton breakers, and places like Badplace Hill and Hell Bay have earned their names through reputation.

Such schizophrenic characteristics make this island special, and a great place to explore. The sandy-beach bays to the island's south are backed by dunes and provide ample opportunity for sunbathing, swimming and snorkelling, although the water can be a little nippy. Just beyond sits Samson Hill, the southernmost point of the island, with far-reaching views across the Scillies. The exposed, heather-covered plateau at the northern end of the island is dotted with prehistoric burial cairns, evidence of Bronze Age settlers. Nearby, the intriguingly-named rock formation of House of the Head may give a nod to the cult of head worship which was popular among Iron Age Celts who used severed heads as bizarre home decorations. Perhaps the recent preference for minimalist interiors helped to put a stop to that particular design craze.

In the centre of this appealing muddle of history and nature is Bryher Campsite, a discreet canvas-only settlement with barely any more environmental impact than the ancient hamlets of this area. With the protection of age-old hedgerows and ramshackle old walls, the site, consisting of four small fields, seems to blend effortlessly into the landscape of the island.

Situated a short climb uphill from the boat jetty, the campsite has elevated views of the harbour, Hangman Island and Tresco, yet occupies a sheltered spot between two higher hills. The ground is fairly level, and the clean, modern facilities, housed in a robust stone building, are excellent.

As with Troytown Farm campsite on neighbouring St Agnes (p18), the appeal of this place is largely due to the splendid isolation and commanding view.

But whereas Troytown feels almost encircled by the Atlantic waves, the elevated, landlocked campsite here at Bryher feels much more connected with the land than the water. Being situated on such a small, sparsely populated island renders the campsite boundaries fairly irrelevant; the entire island belongs to the campers, with plenty of paths to enjoy and open heathland to explore.

It's undoubtedly a beautiful spot, enhanced during the spring months by a profusion of colourful wild flowers, and enlivened in autumn by flocks of migratory birds. In fact, this is a year-round destination for bird watchers, not only for unusual migratory birds stopping off on their way from Northern Europe and the Arctic to Africa, but also as a breeding ground for bright-beaked puffins and clumsy Manx Shearwater, who, despite many years of evolution, are yet to learn how to land without crashing. There are daily boat trips to spot puffins and laugh at Manx Shearwater as they return to the island bird sanctuary of Annet at dusk.

The climate of the Isles of Scilly, which is significantly warmer than that of the mainland, is due to the North Atlantic Drift, a branch of the Gulf Stream which brings warm waters from far-flung Florida. This makes for mild temperatures during the winter months despite occasional fierce gales and high winds. But to really see the best side of this isle of contrasts, visit in the spring or summer when warm, sunny days turn Bryher into an idyllic island paradise.

THE UPSIDE: Location – remote island camping with spectacular views.

THE DOWNSIDE: Location – it's a bit far for the weekend.

THE DAMAGE: £7 per person per night, no dogs.

THE FACILITIES: Excellent toilets, basins and free showers plus coin-operated hairdryer for the ladies and shaver point for the gents. Freezer for ice packs. Coin-operated washing machine and dryer. Tractor service for luggage from the quay (book in advance).

NEAREST DECENT PUB: The cosy Fraggle Rock (01720 422222), Scilly's smallest pub, is just a few minutes' walk down the hill towards the quay. The contemporary Hell Bay Hotel (01720 422947; www.hellbay.co.uk) has an outside bar deck overlooking the sea and outstanding local seafood in the restaurant. Dinner reservations essential.

IF IT RAINS: There isn't much on the island in the way of indoor pursuits. There's a small gallery near the Hell Bay Hotel (Golden Eagle Studio; 01720 422671) or there are culinary diversions at the hotel itself. Otherwise, jump on a boat to visit the larger towns on St Mary's and Tresco.

GETTING THERE: Contact Isles of Scilly Travel (0845 710 5555; www.ios-travel.co.uk) for plane and boat travel or British International (01736 363871; www.islesofscillyhelicopter.com) for helicopter services. Contact Bryher Campsite for luggage pick-up.

OPEN: Mar–Oct.

IF IT'S FULL: There's an equally beautiful campsite on nearby St Agnes (p18).

| Bryher Campsite, Bryher, Isles of Scilly TR23 0PR | t | 01720 422886 | e | bryhercamp@aol.com |

treen farm, porthcurno

Beach babes and sun lovers, oil up and grab your flip-flops – Treen Farm Campsite, three miles shy of Land's End, is just a towel's throw from some of England's finest beaches.

Treen Farm has been in the Halls family for time eternal. During the last war, one of the fields on the cliff top was commandeered by the army as a communications post. A few military buildings were constructed on the land, rendering it useless for farming – but perfect for camping.

Since then, campers and cows have co-existed at Treen Farm and the camping field has been updated. A fancy tap with running water was installed in 1974, and there are now even toilets and hot showers. The spacious site is a comfortable field's length back from the cliff top so isn't overly exposed, but there are sea glimpses over the hedges which gives the site a sense of place.

What you can't see are the beaches, but you don't have to go far. The nearest is Pedn Vounder, a tiny, isolated cove of golden sand accessed by a 10-minute cliff-top walk and a five-minute rocky scramble from the campsite. The difficult position means it's

never busy, but it does get cut off at high tide, so keep an eye on the water. At low tide, you can walk along the sand to Green Bay and the larger Porthcurno beach at the western edge of the bay, a popular family favourite and much more accessible. There's a car park at Porthcurno for day trippers, as well as shops, restaurants and a pub. On a hot summer's day it can be extremely crowded, but the crowds tend not to venture round the bay to the quieter beaches. This stretch of coast is characterised by a series of sharp, triangular coves cut into the grey, granite cliffs, the jagged, weather-lined rocks contrasting with the soft sand beneath. The beaches are sheltered and swim-friendly, with lifeguards on duty at Porthcurno during the summer months.

If that's not enough beach for your buck, it's just 10 minutes in the car to Sennen on the north coast, where Whitesands Bay provides a huge, sweeping arch of yellow, fluffy sand and one of Cornwall's best surfing spots. Bliss. Bucket-and-spade summer days don't come any better than this.

Treen used to be a popular tourist destination thanks to Logan Rock, a 70-tonne lump of granite naturally balanced

such that it could be rocked back and forth. People came from far and wide to try their strength at rocking (or as they used to say, log'n) the stone, until in 1824 testosterone and bravado got the better of a bunch of drunken sailors who pushed it clean over into the sea. Local residents were outraged at this act of mindless vandalism and the ringleader of the sorry gang was ordered by the Admiralty to return the stone to its rightful position at his own expense. It was a project that took considerably more time and energy than the original drunken prank, and nearly bankrupted the young sailor. Needless to say, the rocking action has never been the same since.

Thankfully, modern-day attractions in the area are enough to topple a wobbling rock from its position as principal tourist draw. Aside from the beaches and coastline, diversions include the worthwhile Porthcurno Telegraph Museum telling the story of the first international telegraph system which began its underwater journey here, and the Minack Theatre, an open-air auditorium cut into the cliffs west of Porthcurno. Its dramatic cliff-side setting and the backdrop of the crashing sea makes the Minack a unique theatre experience – and like the fine beaches here, it shouldn't be missed.

THE UPSIDE: Walking distance to outstanding Cornish beaches.

THE DOWNSIDE: No pre-booking.

THE DAMAGE: From £10 for two adults including tent and car; from £13 for family of four. Tents and motorhomes only, no caravans.

THE FACILITIES: Showers (token operated, 25p for five minutes), toilets and washing-up facilities on site. The village shop/café in Treen has most things you might need, including camping essentials, home-made cakes and unpasteurised

Treen Farm milk, straight from the cows. A van selling pizzas sometimes appears at the campsite on a Friday night.

NEAREST DECENT PUB: The Logan Rock Inn (01736 810495) in Treen is a friendly pub selling St Austell Ales and a wide range of meals (£5–£10) including plenty of local fish and seafood options. If it's not the weather for sitting in the flower-colourful garden, try to get a table in the main bar, which has more atmosphere than the food bar.

IF IT RAINS: Indoor attractions abound at Penzance (12 miles) and Land's End (3 miles).

GETTING THERE: Take the A30 southwest from Penzance, then turn onto the B3283 through St Buryan to Treen. The campsite reception is at the shop in the village.

OPEN: Apr–Oct. No pre-booking, just turn up for a pitch.

IF IT'S FULL: Trevedra Farm Campsite (01736 871818) at Sennen is similarly well-positioned for the beach and is popular with surfers. It's 10 minutes' drive from Treen on the north coast.

Treen Farm Campsite, Treen, St Levan, Penzance, Cornwall TR19 6LF | t | 01736 810273

PRIMROSE-
CONCH
50ᵖ

posh and luxurious – the kind of facilities you might expect in a hotel rather than a campsite, all dark wood and steel, mosaic floors, heating and piped music. For first-time campers worried about rickety old loos and cold showers, this place is just perfect – guaranteed to allay any fears. The only problem is then finding other campsites with equivalent luxury.

Everything about this campsite is organised and professional, from the soft-landing children's play area to the outside showers for wetsuits. They've really thought about the guests here, but unfortunately all this luxury comes at a price, and Ayr is one of the most expensive campsites we found.

But when you consider the location of the campsite – just a few minutes' walk from the attractions of St Ives – the price is partially justifiable. Soaking up the enjoyable atmosphere of the town is the main reason for being here, so it's worth paying the extra to be able to come and go at will. Besides, such a peaceful location is rare for an edge-of-town campsite; make the most of it and stroll down the hill to find wide open beaches, trendy bars and cafés, any number of restaurants from chip-cheap fish shops to contemporary fusion affairs, and of course the galleries. For a town steeped in creativity, they've certainly got the art of camping just right.

THE UPSIDE: The views; five minutes' walk to St Ives town.

THE DOWNSIDE: Expensive, and they pack in the punters for peak season, so don't expect much space.

THE DAMAGE: Ouch! Peak season prices are almost double off-season prices. A family of four with a tent and car will pay £27 in summer. Two backpackers in a tent pay £13.50. Detailed price list on the website.

THE FACILITIES: Magnificent showers, plenty of hot water, kiddies playground, electrical hook-ups, laundrette, games room, direct access to coastal path.

NEAREST DECENT PUB: St Ives is full of lovely old pubs including The Sloop Inn (01736 796584), a 14th-century inn right on the harbour.

IF IT RAINS: Don your waterproofs and walk to the Tate St Ives (Porthmeor Beach; 01736 796226).

GETTING THERE: Central St Ives is closed to traffic. Following signs for St Ives from the A30, take the B3311 then B3306 to town, then follow the brown campsite signs to Ayr and Porthmeor

beach. Look out for the entrance at a sharp S-bend in the road.

OPEN: All year.

IF IT'S FULL: Although not in town, Gwithian Farm Campsite (1 Churchtown Rd, Gwithian; 01736 753127) is popular for its proximity to a huge surfing beach. It's about 20 minutes' drive from St Ives.

| **Ayr Holiday Park**, St Ives, Cornwall TR26 1EJ | t | 01736 795855 | w | www.ayrholidaypark.co.uk |

dennis cove, padstow

Cornwall has been savaged by waves. In the 1970s and early 1980s, waves of tourists descended on the Cornish coast for their annual fortnight of fun, emptying their pockets at flashing-light amusement halls and filling themselves dizzy with ice creams and pasties. Then during the 1980s the waves of tourists receded, as people looked further afield to the exotic charms of Spain and beyond. In an age of package discounts and cheap flights, Cornwall just didn't cut it. It was out of favour and out of fashion.

Now, after more than a decade out in the cold, the crowds have returned. Cornwall is once again a sought-after destination and right at the forefront of this Cornish revival was Padstow, a fishing port on the dramatic north coast.

The Padstow success story was helped by its most famous resident, celebrity chef Rick Stein. It all started with The Seafood Restaurant, his award-winning Padstow eatery that quickly gained a reputation for intricate and innovative dishes. Then came his deli, a bistro, a café, a hotel, a posh fish & chip shop down by the quayside and the popular Padstow Seafood School. Stein's mini-empire raised the profile of Padstow,

transforming it into Cornwall's gastronomic capital. It has also altered perceptions of the wider area from a slow backwater to the home of some of the world's best seafood, fresh off the boat. And it's a success story that has encouraged others in the regional tourist industry to look beyond arcades and pasty shops to attract today's sophisticated and demanding holidaymakers.

Even without the flashy food, Padstow is a charming place. At its heart is the busy harbour, buzzing with activity year-round as the fishermen bring in the catch. If you fancy your chances, you can book a boat from the harbour and go mackerel fishing for dinner. A short walk over the headland from the port, you'll find an amazing expanse of sandy beach which opens up at low tide to provide plenty of room for everyone, even on the busiest summer days. This isn't coastal beach but The Camel Estuary – you can see across to the town of Rock on the other side.

Padstow is also the western starting point of the Camel Trail, an easy walking and cycling route that follows the Camel Estuary inland to Wadebridge, then continues alongside the River Camel to

Poley's Bridge. For most of its 17 miles it's incredibly scenic (The Camel Estuary is an area of Outstanding Natural Beauty) and completely car-free, making it a very popular route in summer when hundreds of bikes and cyclists descend on Padstow. The route forms part of The Cornish Way, a huge 200-mile cycle network that criss-crosses the county from Bude to Land's End.

At the start of the Camel Trail, just south of the fishing port, is Dennis Cove campsite. It's a small, well-cared-for family site close to the town and handy for all the attractions. The philosophy here is 'simple camping'; there are just five electrical hook-ups provided for visitors and a well-maintained shower block. Aside from that,

the campsite is essentially two fields of green grass, albeit in a great location and with some commanding views across the Camel Estuary.

The lower field is open all season with trees and hedges providing shelter. It can get a bit squashed down here in the busy months, so a better bet is to make for the upper overflow field, a vast expanse of grass without designated pitch markings. It's further from the amenities and more exposed, being on the higher ground, but the views across the estuary are simply knock-out.

With a barbecue, a bag of fresh Padstow fish and a view like this, who needs posh restaurants?

THE UPSIDE: Glorious views and well-located for The Camel Trail, Cornish Coastal Footpath, beaches and the town.

THE DOWNSIDE: Lower field can be cramped in peak times, with pitches very close together. Not the cheapest site in Cornwall.

THE DAMAGE: Tent, car and two people £11.50–£15.20. Families and couples only, no groups.

THE FACILITIES: Simple amenities block (showers cost extra), dishwashing and laundry facilities. Bicycle hire is available in town.

NEAREST DECENT PUB: The London Inn (01841 532554) on Lanadwell Street does traditional pub grub; The Shipwrights (01841 532451) down by the old harbour is a good place to watch the world go by on a summer's day.

IF IT RAINS: If you haven't made a reservation at The Seafood Restaurant (01841 532700) you could always try St Petroc's Bistro (same number) to escape bad weather. Alternatively, the Eden Project is a 25-minute drive.

GETTING THERE: Entering Padstow on the A389, turn right at Tesco, drive down the hill then turn right onto Dennis Lane and continue all the way to the end.

OPEN: Easter–Sep. Advance booking recommended.

IF IT'S FULL: Next door is the tent-only Dennis Farm campsite (01841 533513), another great site right on the edge of the estuary. There's a boat ramp from the camping ground so it's popular with water-sporters.

Dennis Cove Camping, Dennis Lane, Padstow, Cornwall PL28 8DR   t   01841 532349   w   www.denniscove.co.uk

south penquite

'Diversification' is the buzzword in the farming industry. It's shorthand for 'there's no profit in farming any more, so let's do something else instead.' That's exactly what the Fairman family have done at South Penquite, an 80-hectare farm on the edge of Bodmin Moor.

Dominic Fairman has been the driving force behind the farm's diversification. A farmer who has self-trained in the art of web development, he's built a website to promote the range of attractions now on offer including camping, fishing, school field trips and art days. Even the farming has been transformed. The farm achieved full organic status in 2001 and is an exceptional example of how a smallholding can co-exist with its natural environment with ethical treatment of animals and a traditional crop rotation system that sustains soil fertility.

The care with which the Fairmans conduct their farming is also applied to the campsite. The well-maintained camping fields are just away from the farmhouse, with numbers restricted so they never get overly busy. The unmarked pitches are huge and there's plenty of room for kids to run around. A new pine-clad shower block provides exceptional facilities while staying true to ecological principles. Solar panels on the roof deliver heated rainwater into four family-sized shower rooms lined with recycled plastic bottles and yoghurt pots, so you're doing your bit for the environment just by keeping clean!

The innovation doesn't stop there as Dominic has expanded the camping experience to offer three authentic Mongolian yurts in an adjacent field. The yurts, used by Mongolian nomads for centuries, are vaulted, round-top tents supported by criss-crossing wooden poles that provide a fence-like structure around the circumference. In Mongolia, they cover this with thick felt and animal skins. Here a sturdy canvas material is used to keep out the English elements. In the middle of the roof is a small opening to provide light and ventilation; a skylight for watching the stars at night.

The three yurts at South Penquite are named Daddy Bear (the largest; sleeps six), Mummy Bear (sleeps four) and Baby Bear (sleeps two) and are fully equipped to provide an agreeable balance between 'back to nature' and 'home comforts'. Each has a wood-burner and gas stove for heating and cooking, comfortable futons with throws and cushions for seating and sleeping and all cooking and eating utensils included for convenience.

The yurts provide a very different camping experience. They have the outdoorsy feel of camping, but with the added bonus of being ready for your arrival. Just turn up with sleeping bags and food, and you're all set. It's not exactly luxury camping (you'll still get grubby and have to walk through a field to get to the loo) but it's a complete departure from the usual stay in a tent. For starters, the yurts are quite roomy – you can even stand up. Plus, with central heating, they can be cosy and fun even at cooler times of the year. The experience is enhanced by the pure countryside location of the yurts, right on the edge of the moor. A mapped-out farm walk allows you to explore the area, taking in the ancient woodlands around the farm, Bronze Age hut circles and prehistoric field systems, a standing stone said to have healing powers and the open moorland. There is a spiritual quality to this part of Cornwall, being more remote and unvisited than most areas. One can almost feel the ancient pagan forces at work as the light wind rustles through the trees and the smoke dances in the heavy air, hued by the colours of sunset.

If diversification allows us to rediscover the natural beauty of our countryside, we're all for it.

THE UPSIDE: Mongolian chic on the edge of the moor.

THE DOWNSIDE: Short walk from the yurts to the loos; bring wellies!

THE DAMAGE: Yurts start at £120 per week rising to £260 for the largest yurt in August. Off-peak short breaks are available for half the weekly price. Camping is £4/3 per adult/child.

THE FACILITIES: Good showers and washing-up facilities; yurts come fully equipped, but without bedding. No electrical hook-ups. Farm walk and fishing on site. Bring your own gear.

NEAREST DECENT PUB: As luck would have it, a recent winner of CAMRA's Pub of the Year is within walking distance. The Blisland Inn (01208 850739) overlooks the village green at Blisland and serves tasty real ales as well as basic basket meals. It's a 15-minute walk across the moor from the campsite.

IF IT RAINS: Plenty of options: Eden Project, Blisland Inn, shopping and museums in Truro, Maritime Museum in Falmouth, restaurants in Padstow.

GETTING THERE: Entering Cornwall on the A30, look out for the right turning signposted to St Breward. Follow this road for about three miles until you see the turning for South Penquite on the left.

OPEN: May–Oct.

IF IT'S FULL: Dennis Cove campsite (p40) is at nearby Padstow; it's possible to cycle between South Penquite and Dennis Cove on the Camel Trail.

| South Penquite, Blisland, Bodmin, Cornwall PL30 4LH | t | 01208 850491 | w | www.southpenquite.co.uk |

bay view farm, looe

The story of Bay View Farm begins way back in 1971. A young Cornish cattle farmer called Mike was in need of a decent bull for his herd. He learned of a strong, sturdy specimen for sale at a farm near Looe and went to have a look. When he arrived, he was bowled over – not by the bull, but by the location. The farm and adjacent camping field were perched on a cliff to the east of Looe commanding outrageous views of the coast and across the sea to nearby St George's Island. The place was overgrown and run down, but that just added to its charm. Mike was smitten.

That evening he returned to his young bride Liz to tell her he hadn't bought the bull, but had found a place he could retire to. She gently reminded him it would be 30 years before they could think about retirement, and not to talk such nonsense. Both the bull and the farm were quickly forgotten.

Fast forward to 1999 and the same, slightly older cattle farmer, now sporting grey whiskers, was leafing through *The Cornishman* newspaper when he happened across the very same farm for sale. The auction guide price was too high, but when it didn't sell under the hammer, he approached the vendors.

Call it fate, good fortune or serendipity, Liz and Mike are now the proud owners of Bay View Farm. You can tell they absolutely adore this place by the passion with which they speak about it and the care and attention that goes into its upkeep. For them, it's not a chore to run this campsite, but an opportunity to share this delightful spot with others.

When you see the view, you realise why. It's about as good as it gets on the south coast of Cornwall, with vistas across to West Looe on the far side of Hanner Ford. You can also see across the water to St George's Island, which has a similar story to that of Bay View – someone fell in love with the place and bought it to retire to, in this case a schoolmistress from Surrey and her sister. Although not the most likely candidates to live on a weather-ravaged and remote island with no running water, electricity or other inhabitants, they threw themselves into life on St George's and lived there for many years until they died. Thankfully, they turned down multi-million pound offers for the island from developers and it has now passed to the Cornwall Wildlife Trust who maintain it as a nature reserve.

Back at Bay View, Mike and Liz keep everything just so, from the brand new amenities block to the prize-winning shire horses in the adjacent field. It's not a large site: there are just 12 pitches available to tents, motorhomes and caravans in the camping field, which tilts at an increasingly steep angle towards the sea. Sleep the wrong way and you'll have blood rushing to your head, sleep the right way and you'll be able to enjoy the view in the morning without getting out of bed.

Nearby attractions include Polperro, a quaint and picturesque fishing village with tea rooms, fudge shops and galleries in a car-free higgle-piggle of alleys and narrow lanes. You can also find fresh fish for your barbecue, or if cooking sounds too much like hard work, head to the oldy-worldy Three Pilchards pub by the quay for locally caught fish and tasty ales.

Mike and Liz are certainly very happy at Bay View Farm and are happier still when sharing it with guests. So the story has the perfect ending: two happy semi-retirees, a campsite and a field full of shire horses. No bull.

THE UPSIDE: A good base for exploring a less fashionable but interesting part of Cornwall; a panoramic view.
THE DOWNSIDE: Site is exposed so watch the weather.
THE DAMAGE: £8/£10 per pitch without/with electricity Sep–Jun, £12/£14 Jul & Aug.
THE FACILITIES: Toilets, free hot showers, electrical hook-ups.

NEAREST DECENT PUB: In summer, enjoy the views from the beer garden at the Smugglers Inn (01503 250646), Seaton, just 150 feet from the beach. In winter, head for the snug Three Pilchards (01503 272233), Polperro.
IF IT RAINS: Explore Polperro or the other fishing villages on the coast; the Eden Project is about 10 miles away, near Par.

GETTING THERE: From Plymouth, take the A38 to Trerulfoot roundabout. From here follow signs for Looe on B3253/A387 until you reach No Man's Land, where you bear left to follow signs for the Monkey Sanctuary and then Bay View Farm.
OPEN: Year round.
IF IT'S FULL: Try the nearby sites at South Penquite (p48) or Padstow (p40).

Bay View Farm, St Martins, Looe, Cornwall PL13 1NZ   t   01503 265922 or 07967 267312

tamar valley tipis

The Tamar Valley is the cut of land that divides Devon and Cornwall, a natural border that helped to isolate Cornwall in medieval times when the valley was difficult to traverse. Nowadays, people whiz through on their way down to the Cornish coast, but it's a picturesque area that deserves to be explored in its own right.

The entire region has been designated an Area of Outstanding Natural Beauty due to the rare valley and water landscape that surrounds the Tamar River, Tavy Estuary and Lynher Estuary. Wildlife thrives in the unspoilt environment and the distinctive landscape is punctuated by tall, centuries-old brick chimneys, a sign of its mining heritage. The best way to see the area is to follow the Tamar Valley Discovery Trail, a 30-mile walk that links Plymouth and Launceston and takes in some stunning scenery. Other, shorter circuits offer more leisurely alternatives, where you're never far from a pub or tea room.

In the heart of the Tamar Valley can be found a very different camping experience, just perfect for grown-up kids who never got Cowboys and Indians out of their system. Welcome to Tamar Valley Tipis on Deer Park Farm, a collection of authentic handmade Indian tipis set in a spectacular deep-countryside location overlooking a shimmering pond.

These inverted white cones sprout dramatically from the green foliage; cool canvasses hand-painted with authentic Sioux murals. The intricate, symbolic patterns pay spiritual tribute to the natural elements. Mother Earth is represented by the bottom skirt around the base of the structure with symbols of land and water. The peak of the tipi represents the upper limit of the physical world and therefore depicts Father Sky. Humans, animals and birds are drawn in the area between these two boundaries, completing the unique designs of these colourful temple-homes.

The Indian theme continues inside, with decorative lining painted in traditional tribal designs. Six beds are laid out in time-honoured formation around the circumference of the tent, with a central fire providing heat for cold nights. Thanks to the ingenious air circulation system inbuilt in these tipis, the smoke is sucked out through the hole in the roof, with the sleeping area remaining amazingly smoke free. Each tipi is equipped with an iron trivet for the fire, on which saucepans can be placed for cooking.

A camping stove and a large barbecue pit are also provided, so there are plenty of cooking options. All utensils are supplied, as are pillows and mattresses, so all you need to bring is bedding and food.

The tipis sit on levelled ground with the pond below, and with a view of nothing but countryside. A multicoloured dream-catcher sways in the wind. Smoke trickles out from the top of a tipi. Is this really Cornwall, or have we been transported to the Great Plains?

Unfortunately, Cowboy and Indian costumes are not supplied with the tipis, but there is a chance to dress up at nearby Morwellham Quay, an award-winning living museum that highlights this area's mining heritage. An entire Victorian mining village has been recreated, complete with a smithy, Victorian carriage rides and an underground tramway. They also encourage visitors to borrow the authentic replica costumes and promenade through the village in true Victorian style.

Not many places offer the opportunity to spend a day in Victorian Cornwall, then spend the night in ancient Sioux America. It's like your own personal trip through space and time. Well, we did warn you this area was worth exploring!

THE UPSIDE: Authentic Indian tipis in a countryside location.

THE DOWNSIDE: Only three tipis available.

THE DAMAGE: From £30 per night.

THE FACILITIES: Each tipi comes with everything you need except bedding and food. A separate building hidden behind a hedge has hot showers and flush toilets.

NEAREST DECENT PUB: The Swingle Tree (01579 382395) at Kelly Bray is a friendly country pub serving reasonably priced no-frills meals.

IF IT RAINS: Snuggle up inside the tipi and light a fire! Alternatively, head to the mining museum at Morwellham (01822 832766; www.morwellham-quay.co.uk).

GETTING THERE: From Launceston take the A388 towards Callington. At Kelly Bray turn left onto the B3257 just past The Swingle Tree pub. Turn left at the crossroads towards Luckett, Deer Park Farm is on the left after a mile or so.

OPEN: Jun–Sep.

IF IT'S FULL: North Cornwall Tipis (01840 770254) near Tintagel or Cornish Tipi Holidays (01208 880781; www.tipiholidaysuk.com) at St Kew offer a similar set-up.

Tamar Valley Tipis, Deer Park Farm, Luckett, Callington, Cornwall PL17 8NW

| t | 01579 370292 | w | www.deerparkfarmholidays.co.uk |

croyde bay

Acres of sand, pounding surf and bronzed lifeguards – welcome to the Gold Coast. Not the original Australian Gold Coast, but the North Devon version; slightly cooler, and more importantly, much nearer for us Poms.

There's no disputing the beauty of Croyde Bay, a wide sweep of dune-backed sand flanked by the finest field-green North Devon hills. It's also the nearest thing you'll find to a fair dinkum Aussie surf beach in this part of the world, although the Australian lifeguards on duty would probably disagree, given the difference in temperature between the two hemispheres. The surf is some of the best in North Devon with the full force of the Atlantic swell providing hollow, low-tide waves and rideable beach breaks. It's serious surf, but this beach is popular with beginners as well as experienced surfers thanks to the number of surf shops and surf schools located here.

Along with nearby Woolacombe, Croyde Bay is the venue for North Devon's annual Oceanfest, a freesports and music festival held every year in June, just before Glastonbury. With events including surfing, beach volleyball, kite surfing, skateboarding, BMX jumping and a live music stage, it has grown over the years to become one of the most popular extreme and oceansports events in Europe and helps to give this town its young, lively, surfer-dude atmosphere.

Due to the sheer number of summer visitors, the entire bay seems to turn into one massive campsite during the months of July and August. All the sites are booked up and every spare inch of space is taken by a tent. Many of the campsites in town are small and only open for a month in summer, so we have chosen to mention more than one worthy campsite in the bay.

The pick of the campsites is the small but special Mitchum Meadow, the only site with direct beach views. You can keep an eye on the surf from your tent and run down to the beach when the waves are good. Due to planning restrictions, it's not open all year, but is always open in August. The owner Guy uses another field nearby (Myrtle Meadow) at other times, but it lacks the ocean outlook. Facilities are basic, with spotless portacabin-style showers, which unfortunately spoil the views from the pitches higher up the field. Despite that, it's a magnificent location where you can fall asleep to the sounds of the crashing waves

and dream of being a champion surfer.

Another popular site is Surfer's Paradise, which boasts the nearest position to the beach, just behind the dunes. It's marketed squarely at young surfers and has a reputation for raucous partying so bring ear plugs if you want to sleep at night or an eye mask if you'll be partying all night and sleeping in the day. The site is owned by Ruda, the local campsite conglomerate who also run a giant corporate holiday park in town, where the on-site shopping centre is larger than all the shops in Croyde village combined.

Other campsites include the family-friendly Bay View Farm which has modern facilities but only takes seven-night bookings in peak periods, and the lovely Cherry Tree Farm set on a hill above the village, which is more spacious and has a friendly, relaxed feel.

Despite the summer influx, Croyde village retains its rural charm with traditional thatched cottages, blooming gardens and a suitably old-fashioned post office and village store. Surprisingly, there's also an abundance of tall, swaying palm trees that seem to flourish in this area. Perhaps it is just like Australia's Gold Coast after all…

THE UPSIDE: Beachside location, great for surfers.

THE DOWNSIDE: Small and squashy site; only small tents accepted.

THE DAMAGE: Prices vary; call for details. No pets, caravans, awnings or frame tents.

THE FACILITIES: Good showers and toilets are provided in portacabins. No other facilities on site.

NEAREST DECENT PUB: The Thatch (01271 890349), on the main road through the village, is a lively surfers hang-out with pub food and a good atmosphere.

IF IT RAINS: Surfing doesn't stop when it rains, so don't make excuses – hire boards or organise lessons with Surfing Croyde Bay (01271 891200; www.surfingcroydebay.co.uk) or Point Breaks (07776 148679; www.pointbreaks.com). Check out www.goldcoastoceanfest.co.uk if you're visiting in June.

GETTING THERE: Croyde is about eight miles northwest of Barnstaple. Follow the A361 to Braunton, then take the B3231 into Croyde. Turn left in the centre of the village, then left again onto Moor Lane. Myrtle is just there on the left; Mitchum's is all the way down Moor Lane on the right.

OPEN: Jul (Myrtle) & Aug (Mitchum's) plus other weekends. Call for details about special group bookings.

IF IT'S FULL: Try Surfer's Paradise (01271 890477; www.surfparadise.co.uk), Bay View Farm (01271 890501; www.bayviewfarm.co.uk) or Cherry Tree Farm (01271 890386).

Mitchum Meadow and Myrtle Meadow, Moor Lane, Croyde, N Devon EX33 1NU			
	t	01271 890233	w	www.croydebay.co.uk

lundy island

Lundy Island, a bold outcrop of granite, juts 400 feet into the air from the Bristol Channel. It's just 11 miles from the North Devon coast, but feels more remote than the distance suggests due to the barren, desolate landscape, with its wild, towering cliffs, wind-battered fields and little in the way of trees or shelter. With a permanent population of around 20 in summer and a good few less in winter, it's obviously not the most hospitable of places.

Let's be honest, this isn't camping for beginners. In fact, it probably doesn't sound like the place for camping at all! But despite its bleak, isolated location, camping here can be invigorating and truly spectacular. When the wind drops and the sun appears, this may well be England's most magical camping experience.

As you might expect from its geographic isolation, Lundy has attracted the wrong sort of crowd throughout its history. It was acquired in the 12th century by William de Marisco, a shady character who used it as a base for vicious pirate raids into Devon. During this time, Henry II ceded the island to the Knights Templars of *Da Vinci Code* fame, but they were unable to wrest it from de Marisco. Although he was eventually hanged for his wretched exploits, the island continued as a haven for pirates until around 1750, when it was leased by Thomas Benson, MP for Barnstaple. His activities were suitably worthy of an MP; smuggling and fraud on a grand scale. His favourite scam was to heavily insure a fully loaded ship, secretly unload its cargo at Lundy, then send it out to sea to be burned for the insurance money. The cave used to stash his loot can still be seen underneath the castle, Lundy's oldest surviving building.

Lundy is now managed by the Landmark Trust, an altogether more respectable lot, who maintain the island for the benefit of tourists. They operate a ferry service during summer from Ilfracombe and Bideford, and a helicopter service during winter. They also offer self-catering accommodation on Lundy, but the best way to experience the raw splendour of the island is to camp at the Landmark Trust campsite. Like all the best natural campsites, it's essentially a field with nothing in it, but it has great views around the island over the stone boundary wall and its peaceful, remote location feels a million miles away from the hustle and bustle of modern life.

Unsurprisingly for a small island in the middle of the Atlantic Ocean, it can get windy, so it's important to bring sturdy, hard-wearing tents and robust tent pegs. If you come prepared, you'll be rewarded with a camping experience to remember, with an entire island at your disposal; a maximum of just 40 campers makes for an agreeably tranquil environment.

Activities for the adventurous include walking and climbing, but Lundy is more famous for its world-class diving. Washed by the warm waters of the Gulf Stream, Lundy has some of the richest marine life outside the tropics and has been designated a Marine Nature Reserve. In addition, there are more than 200 shipwrecks, 10 of which are easily accessible, making this one of the best wreck dive sites in the country. For those that just like to splash around, the warden also leads snorkelling safaris during summer.

Whether you come for diving, climbing or just chilling, the focal point on the island is the Marisco Tavern. It never shuts, so at any time of day or night, there's always a place to take shelter and swap stories of tents blowing away in the Atlantic winds. Next door is the island shop, which although small, is amazingly well-stocked – apparently they do a good trade in heavy-duty tent pegs.

THE UPSIDE: Extreme camping on a unique island.

THE DOWNSIDE: Limited water supplies, so maximum 40 campers at any one time.

THE DAMAGE: £6–£10 per night, advance booking essential.

THE FACILITIES: Well-equipped shower block with hot showers and toilets, plus washing machine. The shop and tavern are two minutes' walk from the campsite. No electricity after midnight so bring a torch.

NEAREST DECENT PUB: The Marisco Tavern; not only the nearest pub, but the only pub! Serves tasty food including Lundy lamb and locally caught fish; it's also the place to chat to the islanders or the warden and to check the noticeboard for events.

IF IT RAINS: Time for an extended visit to The Marisco Tavern!

GETTING THERE: The island ship, MS *Oldenburg*, departs from Bideford and Ilfracombe between March and October (adult/child return £47/24).

A helicopter shuttle service runs on Mondays and Fridays during winter (£77/43). Contact the shore office for availability and reservations.

OPEN: Apr–Oct. Winter is a definite no-no for camping, although self-catering accommodation is available.

IF IT'S FULL: There's a great sea-view campsite back on the mainland at Little Meadow (p80), or for island camping alternatives try Troytown Farm (p18) or Bryher Campsite (p22).

Lundy Island Campsite, Lundy Shore Office, The Quay, Bideford, Devon EX39 2LY

| t | 01271 863636 | w | www.lundyisland.co.uk |

little meadow, watermouth bay

The North Devon coast, designated an Area of Outstanding Natural Beauty, is one of Britain's finest landscapes. It has everything: dramatic granite cliffs, wide, sandy beaches and quaint little coves and harbours. At its eastern edge are the green valleys and vast open spaces of Exmoor; to the west, the picture-perfect fishing village of Clovelly.

With such an interesting diversity of landscape, it's not surprising that huge, commercial holiday parks are common in the area. Thankfully, there is also a small, friendly campsite tucked away here, happily minding its own business. It has one of the best views in North Devon, overlooking Watermouth Bay, the Bristol Channel and the cliffs of Hangman Point.

Little Meadow, a modest, unassuming campsite two miles east of Ilfracombe, relies on its position to pull in the punters without having to resort to water slides, amusement arcades and nightly entertainment. Even so, the owners have worked hard to ensure that everyone can enjoy the views from this hillside location by levelling off the land to create a series of terraces. Dividing the campsite like this also means more privacy; you'd never know there are 50 pitches here. The terraces are perfect for camping, being plumb-line level with well-tended soft grass for easy tent-pegging. Bright splashes of roses and dianthus border the pitching areas, framing the view with colour. It's a magnificent spot in which to settle comfortably into a deckchair with a cool beer and to survey the scenery. You might even spy a seal or a basking shark if you're lucky and in possession of a good pair of binoculars.

The owners of Little Meadow have created a low-impact, environmentally friendly site and are quite determined that visitors do their bit too – recycling is compulsory and long, wasteful showers are discouraged by a 20p levy. It's not a chore to get involved, in fact, the 'can-crusher' is great fun and highly addictive, and if people leave with greater awareness of their environmental responsibilities, then it's worthwhile.

Walkers will love the fact that the longest footpath in Britain, the South West Coast Path, runs right past the campsite. The footpath begins at Minehead and closely follows the North Devon shoreline southwest past Little Meadow, on through Cornwall to Land's End, then back along the south coast through Cornwall, Devon and Dorset, ending up near Poole. It's a magnificent walk and

well signposted. The section east of Little Meadow is particularly rewarding as it leads up to the spectacular cliffs of Great Hangman, the highest point on the path at 315 metres. The downside is that it's uphill all the way from Watermouth.

Although you can't see it through the trees from the campsite, the picturesque harbour of Watermouth Cove is directly below. It's a sharp, narrow inlet with a history linked to smuggling, full of small boats at high tide and muddy sand at low tide. Given its proximity to the campsite, it might be worth considering arrival by sea as an alternative means of transport, particularly if the M5 is full of Bank Holiday traffic. Just behind the cove is the solid bulk of 150-year-old Watermouth Castle, now a popular theme park for younger kids. Nearby are the Blue Flag golden sands of Woolacombe, Croyde Bay and Saunton Sands.

The nearest town to the campsite is Ilfracombe, with restaurants, pubs and various tourist diversions including the Landmark Theatre and day trips to Lundy Island (see p76). Apparently, Ilfracombe enjoys some of the highest average year-round temperatures in the UK, confirming that this place really is the coast with the most.

THE UPSIDE: Well-tended terraces providing magnificent ocean views.

THE DOWNSIDE: Facilities are dated and overstretched in summer.

THE DAMAGE: Car, tent and two people £5/9/10 for low/mid/high season.

THE FACILITIES: Hot showers (take some 20p coins) and flush toilets in an old but clean amenities block, hairdryers in each block. Gas and ice pack exchange, basic shop on site selling essentials. Electric hook-ups available. Small, wooded play area for kids.

NEAREST DECENT PUB: Within walking distance, the Old Sawmill Inn (01271 882259) is a perfectly serviceable family pub down the hill near Watermouth Bay. Amongst the tack and tat of Ilfracombe, The Quay (01271 868090; www.11thequay.com) stands out for its wide selection of wines, tasty tapas and its chilled-out vibe.

IF IT RAINS: There's a theatre and cinema in Ilfracombe.

GETTING THERE: Little Meadow is situated between Ilfracombe and Combe Martin. It's about an hour from the M5; leave at J27, take the A361 towards Barnstaple. Just past the South Molton turn-off, turn right to Allercross roundabout (signposted Combe Martin). Drive through Combe Martin; the campsite is 500 metres past Watermouth Castle on the left.

OPEN: Apr–Oct.

IF IT'S FULL: Big Meadow (01271 862282) is another decent spot down near the water's edge at Watermouth Cove. It's a larger site with good views from the higher ground, but there is some traffic noise from the adjacent road.

| Little Meadow, Watermouth, Ilfracombe, North Devon EX34 9SJ | t | 01271 866862 | w | www.littlemeadow.co.uk |

cloud farm, exmoor

Away from the crowds that gravitate towards the popular coast of North Devon, a much quieter side to this county can be found just a short distance inland. Take a drive through Exmoor and the surrounding area, and you'll virtually have the place to yourself. The landscape changes as you move around, from the wild, sweeping open moorland to lush, wooded valleys virtually hidden away from the world. Peace and tranquility can be found in abundance in quaint villages and hamlets, including the immaculate country village of Brendon, where you'd be lucky to see anyone at all – holidaymakers or residents.

A few miles from Brendon, if you know where to look, you'll find the beautiful Doone Valley, a sharp 'v'-shaped incision through the landscape. This is the home of the 110-acre Cloud Farm with a campsite, stables and tea rooms hidden amongst tall pines and steep, purple, heather-clad slopes. The owners, Colin and Jill Harman, have succeeded in creating a relaxed, countryside camping environment. There aren't hundreds of rules to obey, there's no minimum stay in the summer, you can pitch wherever you fancy, and campfires are allowed. Most of the campsite itself is situated on a long, thin strip of land

alongside the Badgworthy Water river. You can choose a pitch by the bubbling brook, or there's another larger field slightly uphill from the river for those who want to spread out.

The farm, at the end of its own road into the valley, is arranged as a small, self-contained hamlet. As well as the old farmhouse, there's a small shop and tea rooms – don't miss out on the cream teas with giant scones almost the size of birthday cakes. The farm stables are home to 32 fine horses, all of which are available for trekking, another good reason to stay at Cloud Farm. This is perfect riding terrain with access to around 11,000 acres of pristine, car-free countryside. Cloud Farm caters for riders of all levels, whether you're after a gentle meander along the lower valley paths, or an exhilarating gallop across the moors. Riders are grouped according to experience with small group sizes of between two and six. You can even bring your own horse; stables and grazing are available for the horse that likes to holiday.

Whether you're exploring Exmoor on horseback or on two feet, you're sure to see a rich diversity of wildlife. This area is home to herons, wild red deer and buzzards

as well as the more common Exmoor pony, said to be closely related to prehistoric horses. You can certainly cover extra ground on horseback, but the walking around here is equally rewarding and you'll see more of the wildlife as you wander along the well-marked paths. A few days riding or walking, and it's easy to see why the Doone Valley has been designated one of only three 'truly tranquil' places in England by the Council for the Protection of Rural England.

Given the magical scenery of the Doone Valley, it's no wonder it was chosen as the setting for one of the most successful romantic novels of all time. RD Blackmore's

Lorna Doone, set in the turbulent time of Monmouth's rebellion in 1685, tells the story of John Ridd, a farmer, who falls in love with the young Lorna Doone and resolves to win her heart and hand. The perennially popular text even mentions Cloud Farm, a claim to fame that still draws Blackmore fans here, although not in any significant number to spoil this area's laid-back charm.

Now, of course, Cloud Farm is featured in an entirely different book, and we can assure you that the beauty of the Doone Valley is strictly non-fiction.

THE UPSIDE: Riverside camping in a hidden valley with on-site horse-riding.

THE DOWNSIDE: Despite a new shower block, still not enough facilities for busy periods, so expect to queue. No mobile phone reception.

THE DAMAGE: Camping from £5 per adult, £3.50 per child. Horse riding £15 an hour.

THE FACILITIES: Hot showers at 50p a pop. Clothes drying and fridge/freezer facilities available. The shop sells groceries, wine,

beer, camping accessories and logs as well as cream teas.

NEAREST DECENT PUB: No outstanding pubs in the immediate area, but the Stag Hunter Hotel in Brendon (two miles away) does the job, and serves everything and chips for £6–£8.

IF IT RAINS: The seaside resort of Minehead is a short drive away as is the medieval village of Dunster with its hill-top castle.

GETTING THERE: From the main A39 Porlock to Lynton road, take the signposted road to Doone Valley and Malmsmead. Turn right at Oare church for Cloud Farm.

OPEN: All year.

IF IT'S FULL: Doone Valley Campsite (01598 741267) in Oare village is a handy option with a similar riverside location, but is very basic and doesn't have the same magical setting.

Cloud Farm, Oare, nr Brendon, Lynton, North Devon EX35 6NU

t | 01598 741234 | w | www.doonevalleyholidays.co.uk

doward park, symonds yat

Symonds Yat village straddles the meandering River Wye in Herefordshire at one of its most beautiful points. As the river sweeps round in a five-mile horseshoe, it cuts a deep gorge into the carboniferous cliffs to form Symonds Yat Rock, a towering limestone outcrop that shoots 500 feet into the air. From the top of the rock, you can survey the breathtaking scenery below, as the river twists and turns its way through the countryside.

The village is actually split into two parts by the river: Symonds Yat West is on the Herefordshire side, with Symonds Yat East on the opposite bank, in Gloucestershire. Although you can see across from one side of the village to the other, they're only linked by road via a circuitous five-mile drive. Pedestrians, however, can travel across by means of an unusual rope ferry. For a small fee, the ferryman will pull visitors across the water using an overhead rope. It's a very old-fashioned way to travel, but befitting for this quiet and pretty little corner of old England.

Of the two banks, Symonds Yat East has the quainter character and more of a villagey feel, with a small, traditional pub, the Saracens Head, overlooking the water.

Back on the west side, a commercial campsite and noisy funfair spoil things a little, but it's just a short climb through the forest to Doward Park, a very peaceful spot to pitch a tent.

Family-friendly Doward Park is a small, terraced campsite surrounded on three sides by dense, wildlife-rich woodland, so it feels more like a forest glade than a conventional campsite. Although securely fenced, the woods are open to public access, providing many fantastic walks. There's also an enclosed section of woodland that forms part of the campsite, ideal for children to explore, make camps and have fun. They might even spot deer as well as badgers and foxes amongst the trees.

The forest-edge location of Doward Park makes it ideal for campers who really want to get away from it all. In fact, it's possible to stay here for a weekend or even a week and not have to use the car at all – there are plenty of things to see and do within easy walking or cycling distance.

The nearest attraction is King Arthur's Cave, a limestone grotto used for shelter long before canvas and guy-ropes were invented. Bones of giant mammoth, woolly rhino, cave

lion and reindeer dating back to the Ice Age have all been found here and remains of early humans have also been discovered nearby.

Other activities within walking distance include canoeing on the deceptively fast-flowing waters of the River Wye, or joining a boat cruise from Symonds Yat to take in the spectacular river scenery. This area is also popular with twitchers, as it's home to the rare and protected peregrine falcon who nest in the cliffs between April and August. You'll often find volunteers from the RSPB on hand at

Symonds Yat Rock to show visitors these birds through powerful telescopes. Further afield, there's plenty of exploring to be done in the Forest of Dean, and it's only a short drive to southeast Wales to see the 13th-century Tintern Abbey or the impressive ruins of medieval White Castle.

But to rush around would be to miss the beauty of this place. Better to make the time to amble around the woods, or sit at the Saracens Head Inn by the river, looking up at the tree-covered gorge, contemplating if this just might be the most peaceful spot in the world.

THE UPSIDE: Peaceful woodland setting near a stunning gorge.

THE DOWNSIDE: No groups accepted. Could do with more showers in peak times. Only 26 pitches, so advance booking essential.

THE DAMAGE: Standard pitch including two adults £10.50/£12.50 low/high season. Motorhomes and tents only.

THE FACILITIES: Two male, two female showers, due for an upgrade. Service washes available for laundry. A small shop on site sells 'everything you might forget' as well as hot drinks including fresh

coffee. There's also an unsupervised children's play area. Canoes can be hired from Symonds Yat Canoe Hire (01600 891069); bikes can be hired from Monmouth Cycle Hire (07782 270114).

NEAREST DECENT PUB: The Saracens Head (01600 890435) at Symonds Yat East is a 16th-century inn. It's only about a mile away, but there is a vertical drop of 350 feet between the campsite and the river. The pub has good food, Theakstons Ales and en-suite accommodation. Watch the noise if you return late to the campsite – a strict 10pm curfew is enforced!

IF IT RAINS: Weston's Cider Farm (01531 660233; www.westons-cider.co.uk) in the village of Much Marcle is an interesting day out, or explore the second-hand book capital of the world at Ross-on-Wye.

GETTING THERE: Doward Park is not far from the A40 between Ross-on-Wye and Monmouth. From Ross, take the exit for Symonds Yat West, then the second exit at the small roundabout and follow the brown signs for Doward Park.

OPEN: Apr–Sep.

IF IT'S FULL: Bracelands (p98) is nearby.

Doward Park Campsite, Great Doward, Symonds Yat West, Herefordshire HR9 6BP

| | t | 01600 890438 | w | www.dowardpark.co.uk |

bracelands, forest of dean

The Forestry Commission certainly know how to run a good campsite. They should; they own over 20 campsites across Britain and some of the finest forest land in the country. With the Forestry Commission, you're guaranteed a site surrounded by woodland, with well-marked forest walks and cycle routes, scenic forest drives, picnic sites and play areas. It's also a good bet you'll have some of Britain's best-kept countryside on your doorstep, with a wealth of rivers, streams, hills and valleys to explore.

Bracelands campsite in the Forest of Dean is no exception. The huge camping meadow on the upper slopes of the Wye valley is surrounded by dense forest on all sides. Even the camping fields, which slope at an increasing angle towards the lower corner, are dotted with the occasional copper beech tree. The view across the valley is of forest too and there are no signs of the 21st century, except within the campsite itself.

The facilities are faultless. Rows and rows of pristine toilets and showers are arranged in three shower blocks, strategically placed around the large site. Of course, there's a genuine need for all these facilities with 520 pitches and up to 2,000 visitors to cater for.

With such big numbers, this site wouldn't suit everyone. In addition, with such a large tree-sparse area cut out of the hillside, it's exposed in windy weather, although there are a few sheltered corners where it's possible to tuck in next to trees and hedges.

On the plus side, there's a partial view of the Wye Valley from some of the pitches. It's not possible to see right down to the meandering river below due to the thick forest, but you can see the cut of the valley and across to the opposite slopes. It's enough of a taster to encourage exploration of the area. An easy walk through the forest and you arrive at the banks of the Wye River, which is passable via the suspension bridge at Bilbins, or you can stay on this side of the river for a lovely walk along to Symonds Yat (p92) or the towering cliffs of Seven Sisters Rock in the other direction.

The Forest of Dean is England's first National Park, but it remains one of the least visited forests, isolated by the Wye and Severn rivers. It differs from most of England's forests being rich in deciduous broadleaved trees such as oak, sweet chestnut, ash and beech rather than the usual evergreen conifers, although there are plenty of those too. About 70,000 cubic

metres (800 double-decker buses-worth) of timber are felled in this forest each year for paper, cardboard, furniture and house-building, but all trees are replaced through planting or natural regeneration. The wood here has been important to England's development throughout history. In Tudor times, Dean oak was used for shipbuilding and helped to establish the country as a dominant sea-faring nation. Legend has it that the Spanish Armada had instructions to destroy the Forest of Dean on landing. Thankfully, they didn't succeed.

The Forest Of Dean Sculpture Trail is a worthwhile excursion, a 3½-mile walk through a particularly beautiful part of the forest, interspersed with sculptures and works of art from different artists. All the installations in some way interpret the forest for the visiting public, but even without pondering the hidden meanings and messages of the artworks, it's a thoroughly enjoyable stroll.

Forest Holidays, who manage all the Forestry Commission campsites, have two other campsites in the Forest of Dean, including Christchurch campsite, virtually next door to Bracelands. While both these campsites may lack seclusion and privacy, there's no faulting them for organisation, facilities and location.

THE UPSIDE: Well-managed campsite in the heart of the Forest of Dean.

THE DOWNSIDE: Colossal site with 520 pitches, so wouldn't suit everyone.

THE DAMAGE: Reception is next door at the Christchurch site. Prices per pitch including two adults start at £7.70 in low season, rising to £11.90. Full details on the website.

THE FACILITIES: Hot and cold water, showers, baby-changing facilities, chemical disposal point, electrical hook-ups, payphone, disabled facilities, dogs welcome. There's a shop next to reception at the Christchurch site.

NEAREST DECENT PUB: The King of Spain (01594 834859) is an okay pub within walking distance of Bracelands. An unpretentious, smoky little place with wholesome grub for about £5 and Greene King IPA, it's on the main road about half a mile from the campsite. It's well worth making the trip to the excellent Saracens Head Inn at nearby Symonds Yat (p92).

IF IT RAINS: Bristol is an easy drive from here; as is the literary town of Ross-on-Wye.

GETTING THERE: From the A40, take the A4136 towards Coleford. Stay on this road until it crosses the B4432 at the Pike House Inn. Take the B4432 towards Symonds Yat then turn left, following the campsite signs. Bracelands reception is at Christchurch campsite, next door.

OPEN: Mar–Oct.

IF IT'S FULL: Christchurch campsite (same contact details as Bracelands) nearby is also run by the Forestry Commission. It's a smaller, sheltered, dog-free site without the valley glimpses of Bracelands, but with even better facilities.

Bracelands, Bracelands Drive, Christchurch, Coleford, Gloucestershire GL16 7NN

	t	0131 314 6505	w	www.forestholidays.co.uk

leela fields

Close your eyes, take a deep breath and open your mind. You'll need an open mind for Leela Fields, an unusual fusion of campsite and New Age healing centre.

Leela Fields campsite is attached to and managed by the Osho Leela Centre, a holistic centre in Dorset that runs a variety of evening and weekend courses. It's named after the revolutionary Indian mystic Osho who, depending on who you talk to, was either a bit of a lunatic or a deeply misunderstood genius. His core message was that there was no message; his core teachings were that there should be no teachings. He opposed the creation of philosophies or ideologies, and reluctantly accepted the role of guru in order to spread his knowledge. And at the centre of this was a very simple thought – that the only thing with any meaning is our own experience in the here and now. He rejected the concept of heaven and earth, reincarnation and the worship of deities, arguing that, in effect we are all gods of our own existence and we should celebrate our lives to recognise that. He encouraged the individual to peel off layers of social conditioning and discover their true self. And that's what the Osho Leela Centre is all about – it's a sanctuary from the restrictions and conditions of everyday life, allowing visitors to experience new things, meditate, explore personal growth and generally loosen up a bit. The principal activity of the centre is the education and training of therapists, but it also offers many courses suitable for everyone from the mildly inquisitive to the fully enlightened. The most accessible of these include regular yoga weekends, meditation courses and healing weekends. Exact programmes vary, but a healing weekend might include four-handed massage, aromatherapy, Indian head massage, reflexology, shiatsu, energy healing and yoga. No experience is required, but you'll be learning how to administer the treatments as well as enjoying them yourself.

These residential courses come with a variety of accommodation options including the basic dorms in the Centre itself, a homely and endearingly shabby gothic structure where you'll also find the dining room and licensed bar. Adjacent to the main building is the campsite and a small number of circular Mongolian yurts used as both treatment rooms and dorms for up to six people. In addition, there are wooden lodges and caravans for hire, and you're welcome to bring your own tent. Leela Fields campsite is also available to visitors who aren't

attending the courses, and consists of two fields – one field busy with lodges and caravans, and another much smaller field in a quieter corner of the grounds, with fantastic views across the green, bowl-top hills of Blackmore Vale and the Dorset countryside. Be warned though, it's a bit of a walk to the facilities from here.

Around the campsite, a nature and conservation park known as the Fields of Play is being developed. A 'Buddha Maze' has been planted which, when fully grown, will become a Buddha-shaped labyrinth of trees and hedges. A tiny Buddha statue sits in a clearing at the centre of the maze, an ideal spot for some quiet meditation.

A small orchard has been planted with seven rows of seven fruit trees, geometrically spaced according to the principles of Feng Shui. To add to the calming ambiance, an oval lake is being prepared and a planned sensory garden will allow both sighted and non-sighted visitors to enjoy the delicate touches and smells of nature. The overall aim of the Fields of Play is to create a soothing environment to aid meditation and relaxation.

There's no doubt, a weekend here is good for the soul and the spirit, giving visitors an opportunity to shed all the baggage of their materialistic lives and regenerate the inner self. Camping with added karma.

THE UPSIDE: Camping holiday for mind, body and spirit.

THE DOWNSIDE: Some of the attractions in the Fields of Play are not yet finished.

THE DAMAGE: Camping from £5 per night, wooden lodges from £135 for a short break, healing weekends from £70. Yurt prices and availability vary according to the events and courses at the centre. Call for details.

THE FACILITIES: Modern amenities block includes facilities for disabled guests.

No shop on site. Gillingham town centre is only a five minute drive.

NEAREST DECENT PUB: Plenty of pubs to choose from in Gillingham, including The Phoenix (01747 823277) on the main shopping street, serving a good pint of the excellent Badger Beer.

IF IT RAINS: If you're not on one of the courses at the Centre, there's a leisure centre in Gillingham, or you could take a drive to see Stonehenge.

GETTING THERE: From M3 junction 8, take the A303 until Mere then the B3092/5 to Gillingham. Follow the brown camping signs until the traffic lights at the B3081. Turn right, then left after 100 metres into Broad Robin which becomes Common Mead Lane. Thorngrove/Leela Fields is on the right after about 1/4 of a mile.

OPEN: Yurts and lodges available all year; camping Apr–Oct.

IF IT'S FULL: This is the only camping/meditation centre that we know of in the UK; if it's full, relax, take a deep breath and choose another date.

Leela Fields, Thorngrove House, Common Mead Lane, Gillingham, Dorset SP8 4RE

| t | 01747 821221 | w | www.leelafields.co.uk and www.osholeela.co.uk |

tom's field, langton matravers

In an area of rural coastal Dorset called the Isle of Purbeck, which isn't actually an island, it seems appropriate that Tom's Field Campsite isn't in fact Tom's. It was at one stage, but Tom has now pitched his tent in that great campsite in the sky, leaving his field to be loved, nurtured and camped on by younger generations.

If it isn't Tom's, it is at least a field, so that part of the description is accurate. It's rather a nice field, comprising just over four acres of gently rolling soft grass with old stone walling around much of its perimeter. It's divided into a flat lower field, and a slightly more undulating higher field, which is compensated for by the outlook. If you're looking the right way, you can see a long view seaward across Swanage Bay, and on a clear day you might even see the Isle of Wight. It's a lovely outlook to wake up to; enough to make you want to jump into the car and go exploring.

With so many attractions around here, it's difficult to know where to start. The pub is probably as good a place as any, and what a pub the Square & Compass in Worth Matravers is. For a start, it's an anti-tardis: it looks quite large from the outside, but once inside, it's unbelievably tiny with just a couple of pokey little rooms with half-height ceilings. Unusually for a pub, there's no bar, just a little hatch opposite the front door, where normally you might be inclined to offer your coat in exchange for a cloakroom ticket. But here good ales by the pint and good pasties by the dozen are served. It's such a gem of a pub, it has become an attraction in its own right, with visitors making a special trip to Worth Matravers to taste the ales and pasties, sit by the fire and bang their heads on the low beams.

By way of an excuse to visit the Square & Compass, Worth Matravers serves as the starting point for some great walks in the area. From here you can link up with the Purbeck Way and the South West Coast Path. A popular walk takes you along the dramatic coastline to Lulworth Cove and on to the much-photographed natural sculpture of Durdle Door, a grand stone arch straddling the sea, weathered out of Portland stone.

This entire stretch of coast is now a UNESCO World Heritage Site due to the geologically significant sedimentary rocks which date back more than 100 million years. The remains of an ancient fossil

forest can be found east of Lulworth, and dinosaurs were known to have been active along this shoreline, giving rise to the name Jurassic Coast.

The nearest town to Tom's Field is Swanage, a relaxed seaside resort with a swim-safe sandy beach and plenty of fish & chip shops. Also nearby is the village of Corfe Castle, a pretty stone settlement in the shadow of the romantic ruins of the castle of the same name. All tea rooms and trinket shops, it's an idyllic village in which to while away an afternoon.

Visit in summer to enjoy Studland Bay, one of England's finest beaches with over three miles of glorious sands lovingly maintained by the National Trust. There are sections clearly marked for both naturists and clothes-wearers, so watch out for the signs to be sure to end up in the right place.

As a World Heritage Site, this coastline has joined the likes of the Great Barrier Reef and the Grand Canyon as one of the wonders of the natural world. Tom would be proud.

THE UPSIDE: Relaxed campsite with views of Swanage Bay and the Isle of Wight.

THE DOWNSIDE: Can be overcrowded at peak times rendering the shower facilities inadequate – choose your time to visit carefully. Advance bookings not generally accepted.

THE DAMAGE: Tent, two people plus car £7.50–£8. No caravans.

THE FACILITIES: A chilly toilet block with showers (20p tokens), washing-up facilities, disabled facilities, a well-stocked shop and gas exchange.

NEAREST DECENT PUB: As well as the quaint Square & Compass (01929 439229) in Worth Matravers which is a five-minute drive or a half-hour walk from the campsite, there's another excellent pub in nearby Kingston called the Scott Arms (01929 480270) with a delightful pub garden and views of Corfe Castle.

IF IT RAINS: Pick up the free 'Swanage & Purbeck' guide at the campsite shop for local attractions, or get the car ferry across Poole Harbour to explore Poole and Bournemouth.

GETTING THERE: Leave the A35 onto the A351 or A352 (depending on direction) and proceed for 11 miles. Turn right onto Haycrafts Lane; after a mile turn left onto the B3069 and after another mile turn right onto Tom's Field Road.

OPEN: Mar–Oct.

IF IT'S FULL: A similar, simple set-up at Burnbake Campsite (01929 480570; www.burnbake.com) is located in a pleasant woodland setting just a few miles away.

Tom's Field, Tom's Field Road, Langton Matravers, Swanage, Dorset BH19 3HN				
	t	01929 427110	w	www.tomsfieldcamping.co.uk

roundhill

In a land of rules, regulations, road-markings and traffic lights, the New Forest in Hampshire offers, both literally and metaphorically, a breath of fresh air. Meandering roads go where nature tells them, following the lie of the land. The road edges gently disappear into the forest, with not a yellow line or a curbstone in sight. Horses wander freely around this wooded landscape, grazing on the roads if they so choose. They have right of way here; traffic just has to live with it.

There's something quite liberating about this arrangement. It's as if in a very small way, we're acknowledging that nature is the greater force here. We're merely humans, visiting for a time, borrowing these natural resources. In the New Forest, instead of dominating nature as we usually do, we're living alongside it. And it all works very well.

If you can dodge the horses as far as Brockenhurst, you'll find one of the Forestry Commission's most outstanding campsites, Roundhill. Once an airfield, it's now a large expanse of open heathland right in the middle of the forest, with trees and shrubs breaking up this huge area to create smaller, sheltered pockets of land. There are no designated pitches; just drive around for a while, find an agreeable spot and as long as you're at least 20 feet away from the nearest tent, it's all yours.

The campsite is well laid out and well organised, so it's worth familiarising yourself with the layout of the park before you claim a particular tent-sized piece of forest. Where you pitch will be a function of your preference for company or solitude, forest or open space, and whether you want to walk or drive to the facilities. Everyone is catered for, including those not particularly keen on dogs – there's a sizeable dog-free area at the back of the campsite with some prime pitches amongst the trees. Other places to note include the lakeside area near reception and the adjacent pine woods, both popular locations with regulars.

As with everywhere else in the New Forest, animals have grazing rights here, so expect to see horses, donkeys, cows and even pigs wandering freely around the campsite. For the most part, they keep themselves to themselves, content to watch these strange-looking campers going about their business. If they get wind of your food however, it's a different story. The donkeys are highly skilled at unzipping tents with their mouths

and helping themselves to whatever they can find. Rumour has it they can even open ring-pulls on cans! The trick is never to encourage them by feeding them and always keep food locked in the car rather than in the tent.

Other than the obvious attractions of exploring the New Forest by car, on foot or on horseback (maps and information available at reception), Roundhill is perfectly located for the National Motor Museum at Beaulieu, a fantastic collection of historic vehicles including the World Record Breakers *Bluebird* and *Golden Arrow*. Other exhibits include the *James Bond Experience*, where you can see a number of Q's inventions, including the road-boat from *The World Is Not Enough*. Look out for various events here, including a regular farmers' market, where you can buy fresh New Forest produce.

In an area where cars come second to nature and horses rule the road, it's entirely appropriate to see cars relegated to the status of artefacts at a motor museum. The balance of nature has been restored.

THE UPSIDE: Forest camping with added animals.

THE DOWNSIDE: With all those animals, be careful where you tread! A further downside is that up to 2,000 people can be camping here in peak periods.

THE DAMAGE: From £6.90 to £13.70 per unit (up to four people) per night.

THE FACILITIES: Hot and cold water, washing cubicles, flush toilets, chemical disposal point but NO SHOWERS. At the helpful reception desk you can buy batteries, tent pegs, maps, bread and milk.

NEAREST DECENT PUB: The Filly Inn (01590 623449), back on the main A337 Leamington Road at Setley is 10 minutes in the car. It's an appealing old-style pub with low oak beams, plenty of tankards and brass paraphernalia on the walls plus traditional pub grub (mains £8–£14).

IF IT RAINS: The National Motor Museum (01590 612345; www.beaulieu.co.uk) is open every day from 10am until 5 or 6pm.

GETTING THERE: From the B3055 at Brockenhurst, turn onto the Beaulieu road and head east for two miles.

OPEN: Mar–Oct.

IF IT'S FULL: Nearer to the village of Brockenhurst is Hollands Wood (0131 314 6505), another equally impressive Forestry Commission campsite with the added bonus of hot showers. The downside is the proximity to the main road.

Roundhill Campsite, Beaulieu Road, Brockenhurst, Hampshire SO42 7QL

| | t | 0131 314 6505 | w | www.forestholidays.co.uk |

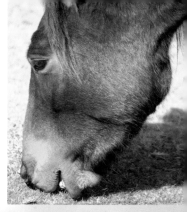

grange farm

The Isle of Wight is undergoing something of a transition. It's shaking off a reputation as one giant island retirement home and adopting a younger, more vibrant image. At the forefront of this is the realisation amongst England's surfing community that the Isle of Wight has some exceptional waves, and for many, it's quicker and easier to access than Devon and Cornwall. It's not just surfing either; kite-surfing, paragliding and some great summer music festivals are also attracting a new crowd.

The Isle of Wight is shaped like a front-on cow's head. At its temple is a town appropriately enough called Cowes. To either side, at the cow's ears, are the towns of Yarmouth and Ryde, both of which have regular ferry services to the mainland. Beneath the ears, the long jaw and chin of the cow is the south coast, home to the island's best surf spots.

Depending on conditions, you might find some worthwhile waves at Sandown and Shanklin. Freshwater and Niton are for experienced surfers, while Compton Bay, on the southwest coast, is where you'll find consistent waves breaking onto a sandy beach, providing suitable surf for all levels. It's the most popular place to surf on the island, but unlike Devon's finest surf spots, rarely gets overcrowded. There's more than enough room to share this water with wind-surfers and kite surfers, who sometimes even outnumber those powered only by waves.

Compton is also a popular launching site for paragliders, who take advantage of the high cliffs and smooth flying conditions. At least two local schools offer tuition here and at another dozen or so launching sites along this stretch of coast. If you fancy jumping off a cliff with something that looks like half a tent on a piece of string, High Adventure Paragliding School (01983 752322) has a variety of courses, from one-day tasters to a full week's Pilot Licence training.

The next bay down from Compton is Brighstone, another sandy beach backed by tall sea cliffs. Perched on top of these cliffs is Grange Farm campsite, a flat, grassy field that goes all the way to the edge of the cliff. You decide how near to the edge you want to pitch – as well as strength of character, you'll need a sturdy tent due to the high winds that can blow in from the sea. The reward is a panoramic, uninterrupted view across the ocean, a lungful of unpolluted sea air, and an easy scramble down to the beach below.

The campsite has deliberately been left as undeveloped as possible for visitors to enjoy the natural beauty of this dramatic coast. There's no café or entertainment, but there is a small shop and kids can entertain themselves by getting to know the farm animals including Rodney and Delboy, the resident llamas.

The picturesque thatched-cottage village of Brighstone is just half a mile away, and has a shop, pub and tea rooms. A National Trust museum, housed in a row of these cottages, recounts the history of this age-old island community.

If Brighstone represents the island of old, Bestival (p246) represents the new. It's an innovative dance-music festival that's proving to be the hot-ticket in England's summer festival calendar. It joins the recently revived Isle of Wight Festival in helping to redefine what this island is all about.

As more visitors begin to know the Isle of Wight as a destination for big-name festivals, world-class surfing, windsurfing and kite-surfing, unparalleled paragliding and general fun and tomfoolery, it may eventually lose its image as a pensioner's paradise. It's already more Blue Crush than blue rinse. Definitely not for granny.

THE UPSIDE: Cliff-top pitches with panoramic sea views and easy access to action and adventure.

THE DOWNSIDE: Exposed location, so expect high winds. Minimum four-night stay at peak times. All the rules and notices everywhere are a bit unnecessary.

THE DAMAGE: Two people, car and tent £11–£13.

THE FACILITIES: Free hot showers, flush toilets, washing-up facilities in heated block. The coin-operated bath and family washroom are nice touches. Launderette, hairdryers, phone and drinks machine also on site.

NEAREST DECENT PUB: The Three Bishops (01983 740226) in Brighstone is so bad it's worth a visit, with unimaginative food, tacky paper napkins and regular bingo nights. A better alternative is the beer garden at The Blacksmiths Arms (p136).

IF IT RAINS: The main town is Newport, worth exploring in wet weather, but the island claims to have more sunshine than anywhere else in the UK, so it shouldn't be a problem!

GETTING THERE: From Fishbourne/Cowes follow signs to Newport then Carisbrooke. At Carisbrooke take the A3323 to Shorwell and Brighstone. Just before Brighstone, turn left by

the church and follow New Road all the way to the end. Grange Farm is opposite. From Yarmouth, follow signs to Freshwater Bay, then follow the A3055 for five miles, looking out for Grange Farm on the right. For ferry crossing information, see p136.

OPEN: Mar–Nov.

IF IT'S FULL: For a cheap, basic surfer's campsite near the beach at Compton, head to Compton Farm (01983 740215), a working farm in a sheltered valley. A great countryside location and a short walk to the beach.

Grange Farm, Brighstone Bay, Isle of Wight PO30 4DA

| t | 01983 740296 | w | www.brighstonebay.fsnet.co.uk |

vintage vacations

God bless America, home of the free. And of the trailer.

We can only be grateful that the US does everything so much McBigger and McBetter, because without that super-sized can-do attitude, we might never have experienced one of America's best inventions – the slick, stylish Airstream trailer. It's an incredible feat of engineering and a joy to behold, with effortless, curved lines, a sparkle of silver and a spacious, luxurious interior. This is no ordinary caravan – it's style on wheels.

Built from as early as the 1920s, the Airstream really took off with the popularisation of leisure travel during the post-war boom. It soon became the standard for luxury camping: Hollywood stars demanded them on set and Armstrong and his fellow astronauts even stayed in an Airstream when they returned from their little jaunt to the moon. The publicity helped to establish the brand nationwide, and the Airstream became an American icon.

The early riveted aluminium trailer was replaced by more modern motorhomes from the 1980s, but the sturdy construction and timeless design of the original has led to a

renaissance for these classic caravans. They've gradually been appearing in trailer parks and movie sets in the States in recent years. Perhaps more unexpected is to see two particularly fine examples in a small field near Newport on the Isle of Wight.

This is the home of Vintage Vacations, brainchild of photographer Frazer Cunningham and stylist Helen Carey. Their love for all things retro compelled them to import two of these beautiful caravans, a 1965 Tradewind and a 1971 Safari. The exteriors were in mint condition but they restored the tired interiors, staying as faithful as possible to the mid-century origins. The result is a perfect blend of holiday comfort and retro chic.

The Tradewind is the original 1960s glamour van, its high-shine aluminium exterior pinging with colourful reflections. You can almost imagine Marlon Brando or James Dean stepping out from the curve-top door, smoking a cigarette and throwing a moody look in your direction. Inside, the 1960s theme continues with yellow-lacquered kitchen cupboards, colourful curtains and rock 'n' roll CDs, as well as retro games including Tiddlywinks and Fuzzy Felt.

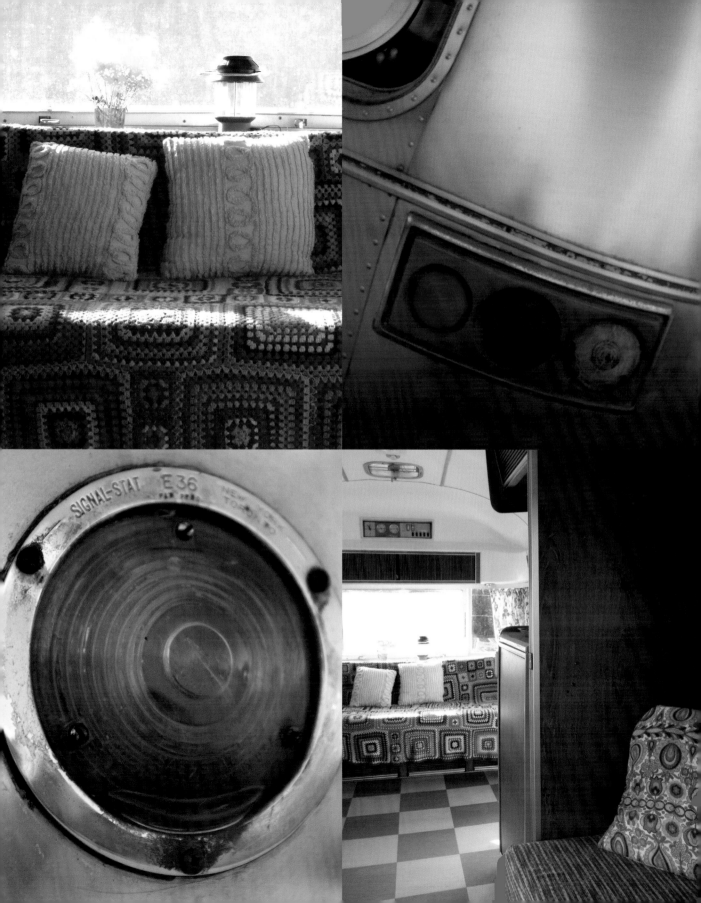

The Safari reflects a more sophisticated era, with a brushed-metal exterior, a hi-tech retractable step for the climb aboard and dark-wood panelling completing the look inside. With complimentary Babycham and appropriate music, it's like a giant metallic time capsule.

When you're ready to return to the present day, you'll find the usual holiday diversions at Newport, the island's biggest town, just 10 minutes in the car. You could take in a show at the historic Apollo Theatre, visit the farmers' market on a Friday morning or hang out at the Quay Arts Centre, a thriving gallery, café and live arts venue housed in a former warehouse on the riverbank.

Helen and Frazer love life on the Isle of Wight, having recently moved here from London to concentrate full time on Vintage Vacations. They're planning to grow the business from its current, temporary location in a field on a working dairy farm. The aim is to import more trailers and eventually open a small caravan park made up entirely of classic caravans and trailers from around the world. For the moment, there are just the two trailers, each comfortably sleeping four people. For visitors or larger groups, an additional tent can be hired by the night – retro floral print, of course.

THE UPSIDE: A unique and memorable camping experience in a shiny bubble of fun.
THE DOWNSIDE: Only two trailers available at present, so difficult to get a reservation.
THE DAMAGE: From £135 per trailer for a short break; from £300 for a week.
THE FACILITIES: Fridge, cooker, toaster, well-equipped kitchen, shower/bath, linen and towels, radio, CD, hairdryer, Fuzzy Felt, Tiddlywinks. Toilets are in the adjacent farmhouse.

NEAREST DECENT PUB: Many options in nearby Newport but for a great view across the island and out to the Solent, head to the beer garden at The Blacksmiths Arms (01983 529263) in Calbourne on the main Newport to Freshwater road. Good Sunday lunches plus guest ales.
IF IT RAINS: Newport has everything including some traditionally tacky holiday favourites – a Waxworks Museum and Waltzing Waters, a water and light spectacular set to music. There are also great tea rooms everywhere on the island.

GETTING THERE: Detailed directions are supplied on confirmation of booking. For ferry information, contact Wight Link (0870 582 7744; www.wightlink.co.uk) or Red Funnel (0870 444 8898; www.redfunnel.co.uk).
OPEN: Mar–Oct (full week bookings only during Jul & Aug).
IF IT'S FULL: There's no substitute for these classic caravans!

| **Vintage Vacations** Newport, Isle of Wight | t | 07802 758113 | w | www.vintagevacations.co.uk |

blackberry wood

There's something of the hippie in Tim and Eva, the young owners of Blackberry Wood, and as at all good family-run campsites, their personalities are reflected throughout this very special place. Nestled in the foothills of the South Downs and blending effortlessly into the native woodland, it's part family campsite, part upmarket hippie playground.

Near the entrance to the campsite a small, flat field accommodates an odd assortment of permanent caravans, some of which are available to hire. The centre of the field is a large play area where Tim occasionally lights a big bonfire and maybe a barbecue, a warm focal point of entertainment and sociability for colder evenings.

Behind this field is Blackberry Wood, a rambling straggle of trees and thicket, with a few tentative footpaths criss-crossing through the undergrowth. Campers can choose one of 20 individual clearings dotted around the dense woodland. Each spot has its own unique personality and most have been named by previous occupants, inspired by the character of the location. Some more obviously named hideaways include Fruity in the shade of a crab apple tree, Minty with its gloriously fresh-smelling herbs, Hawthorns and Bramble Hide. A popular spot is Avalon, a large and beautifully shaded clearing, an oasis of calm in the hotter summer months. Then there are the more eclectically christened Boho, Wobble and Aroha, the latter of which means *love* in Maori, and has benefited from an authentic Maori blessing. These delightful clearings allow campers to really get amongst nature and, without sounding too hippified, reconnect with the earth.

To the element of earth is added another pagan element – fire. As more and more campsites refuse to allow campfires, it's refreshing to find a place that positively encourages them. There's something quite magical about being able to fall asleep by a crackling fire in your own woodland clearing. It's like having the best room in a hotel – the woodland suite, perhaps. Except here the roaring log fire doesn't need a chimney, and there's no room service. Logs are available at the house.

While we're on the subject of elements, water is important here too – saving water, that is. Environmentally-minded Tim hasn't installed a flashy facilities block. Campers use a small, old-fashioned but highly characterful hut with hot showers and prominent notices requesting the responsible use of water.

BLACKBERRY WOOD
CAMPSITE • WELCOME!
<PARKING • RECEPTION>

esterel

Blackberry Wood is very much alive with nature; the birds are full of song and the bunny rabbits are full of energy. Even the trees that have been felled by the wind and weather continue to grow horizontally, creating a remarkable living sculpture to admire and a crazy playground to scramble about on.

Once you're finished exploring the woods, you can strike out across the South Downs. Well-kept footpaths and bridleways allow miles of country walking uninterrupted by roads or cars. Depending on which direction you go, a 45-minute walk can take you to the village of Ditchling with its museum and tea room; to the superb Jolly Sportsman pub with outstanding food and ambiance; or to the Black Cap viewpoint, a high point on the South Downs Way from where you can see eight miles across the Sussex countryside to the sea. As always, Tim and Eva have thought of everything, and have drawn up maps of the area, marking all the walks, pubs and other attractions.

All in all, this tiny, unpretentious campsite is one of the best in England, due to the simple fact that untouched nature is valued more highly than comfort and commerciality. And that's exactly what a campsite should be about. It also has the four essential elements that make up a truly great site – earth, fire, water and an exceptional local pub.

THE UPSIDE: Back-to-nature woodland camping with a pagan vibe.

THE DOWNSIDE: Hard to find a bad word to say about this site. Bring wellies in case it rains!

THE DAMAGE: Charges are £5 per tent plus £5/£3 per adult/child. Advance booking essential.

THE FACILITIES: Hot showers, flush toilets, washing-up facilities, barbecue pits. Logs for sale.

NEAREST DECENT PUB: As if the idyllic setting isn't enough, there's a truly great pub within walking distance. The Jolly Sportsman (01273 890400; closed Sun evening and Mon) in East Chillington is fantastically snug and cosy and serves up a changing menu of gastro delights including roast guinea foul and Ditchling lamb with spiced aubergine (mains £12–16).

IF IT RAINS: It's only eight miles to Brighton with its Pier and Pandora's box of attractions. For a more chilled out vibe, make for Lewes, five miles southeast of the campsite.

GETTING THERE: From the M23 continue south onto the A23 for 14 miles. Turn left onto the A273 for about one mile, then bear right onto B2112 New Road for two miles. Turn right onto the B2116 Lewes Road and turn left onto Streat Lane after two miles. You'll see the campsite signposted on the right.

OPEN: Apr–Sep.

IF IT'S FULL: There's always plenty of room at Southdown Farm (01273 843278; www.southdown-farm.co.uk) in Hassocks, a traditional farm campsite with countryside views.

Blackberry Wood, Streat Lane, Streat, nr Ditchling, East Sussex BN6 8RS | t | 01273 890035

the warren

The soaring white cliffs of Folkestone and nearby Dover are iconic; a symbol of England's grand coastline and a natural defence against the wild sea and invading troops. They're often the last thing travellers see when leaving England and the first, welcoming sight on returning home. The cliffs have witnessed it all – wars, crazy cross-Channel attempts and underwater tunnels – and through it all, they have stood firm and strong, a reliable constant in a changing world.

Thankfully, no hotels or other buildings are permitted along this cliff edge, but there is one spectacular location, just east of Folkestone, where you can pitch your own room with a view at the foot of the cliffs.

The Warren, operated by the Camping and Caravanning Club, is perhaps their best-located site in England. Set in a particularly attractive curve of the Kentish coast, it has an outlook of Channel waters and chalky crags. It's also one of the closest spots to continental Europe, which makes it handy for a ferry or Channel Tunnel excursion. It's said that you can even see France from your tent on a clear day.

The main camping field is a pristine strip of grass with flat, marked pitches. Those at the end nearest reception are more exposed and have direct views across the Channel. At the furthest end there's more shelter, but at the expense of the sea views. There are also a few special hideaways – tiny little pitches tucked away amongst the trees for just one or two tents – including the secluded Honeymoon pitch.

The facilities at the site are good. There are two well-equipped shower blocks with four showers in each, just enough for this smallish campsite. There's also a family room, disabled facilities and a laundry. There's no shop as such, but you can buy ice creams and other essentials at reception and order newspapers for the morning. Unfortunately, they don't deliver them to the tents…

A path leads down from the campsite to the shingle and sand beach below. Next to this, an odd-looking concrete platform spoils the natural order somewhat. It was originally built to protect the cliffs from further erosion, but now provides a good spot for fishing or for kids to explore the rock pool-like puddles left behind by the retreating waves. On the far side of the platform, a sandy beach spreads out along the base of the cliffs.

Whereas the white cliffs here are long-lasting symbols of England's grand heritage, the nearby nature reserve of Samphire Hoe, between Folkestone and Dover, is the very newest part of England. When the Channel Tunnel was built, millions of tonnes of excavated earth had to find a new home, so it was decided to extend England into the sea. The chalk marl was dumped at the foot of the Shakespeare Cliff, reclaiming the land and creating this nature reserve, an intriguing other-world landscape of chalky earth, salt-water pools, fescue grasses and wild flowers. The reserve attracts an incredible diversity of plants, birds and other wildlife, including the human variety: walkers, picnickers and sea-anglers all use this peaceful place to enjoy the magnificence of the cliffs.

You can walk right along the cliffs from The Warren to Dover, a good day's walk at a healthy pace. For a shorter stroll on the most stunning section, head to Langdon Cliffs, east of Dover, where an interesting Visitor Centre explains how these cliffs were formed. The melting ice caps that covered Northern Europe more than half a million years ago forced their way through the land mass, splitting England from France, creating the English Channel, these mighty cliffs and, in the process, one of England's best camping spots.

THE UPSIDE: White-cliff coastal camping. Handy stopover for trips to France.

THE DOWNSIDE: Exposed pitches in windy weather; long walk to pub.

THE DAMAGE: Low season prices are £4.30/£1.90 for an adult/child; high season £7.40/£2.00. Tents and motorhomes only. No caravans.

THE FACILITIES: Toilets, showers, family shower room, washing-up sinks, laundry, chemical disposal point.

NEAREST DECENT PUB: It's a 45-minute walk into Folkestone, although the pubs there don't have much to recommend them. Ask at the campsite for directions to walk up the cliff to The Lighthouse (01303 223300) in Capel-le-Ferne where you can enjoy a pint of Ramsgate No 5 and views out across the sea.

IF IT RAINS: Dover Castle, an impenetrable fortress overlooking the town, is well worth a day trip. There's not much of note in Folkestone itself, although they promote their wide, sweeping promenade and cobbled high street as attractions. Fresh fish can be bought at Folkestone harbour.

GETTING THERE: From the M20 J13, take the A20 towards Dover for a short way until it crosses the A260. Follow the A260 towards Folkestone, then turn left onto Hill Road, following signs for 'Country Park'. At the junction of Dover Road, turn left then immediately right, onto Wear Bay Rd. Take the second turning on the left and follow the track for half a mile to find The Warren. Arrivals after 8pm by prior arrangement only.

OPEN: Apr–Oct.

IF IT'S FULL: Also accessed from Wear Bay Road is Little Switzerland Campsite (01303 252168). It's tarnished by static caravans, but the terraced tent pitches are set in beautiful alpine-like scenery.

The Warren, Wear Bay Road, Folkestone, Kent CT19 6NQ

| t | 01303 255093 | w | www.campingandcaravanningclub.co.uk |

orchard camping

'UFO lands in Suffolk – and that's official' ran the front-page tabloid headline. As details emerged, the sensational story gripped the nation and sane and balanced people began speculating that maybe, just maybe, there was something Out There.

It was 1980, and a group of American airmen based at Woodbridge US Airforce Base near Ipswich were out investigating reports of a strange object that had appeared to crash into trees. They approached the location in Rendlesham Forest, Suffolk, when suddenly they were confronted with what appeared to be an alien spaceship – an oval-shaped object with red glowing lights – hovering above the ground. As they approached the spaceship, it sped off at supernatural speed. Landing marks were seen on the ground, burns were found on nearby trees and evidence of radiation was recorded.

The incident – a highly significant sighting backed-up by credible witnesses and documented in a report by the Deputy Base Commander – became known as the 'British Roswell' and Rendlesham Forest became the focus of UFO research in the UK.

Whether truth or myth, the legend that surrounds the encounter grows stronger, and believers and watchers from all over the world continue to visit the site to draw their own conclusions about what really happened that night. The Forestry Commission organise guided UFO walks from the Rendlesham Forest Centre during summer, and there's even a regular, optimistically named *Alien Encounter Weekend* held at Orchard Camping in Wickham Market, just a few miles from the alleged sightings.

Visitors to Orchard Camping are more likely to hail from inner London rather than outer space, as it's only two hours from the capital, but it is worlds away from the city bustle. The main camping area is a simple paddock with plenty of well-tended grass and a scattering of apple trees. At the lower end of the gently undulating field, there's a denser section of woodland where you can find seclusion amongst the mature trees. A small river forms the border of the site at this edge.

A major factor in the attraction of Orchard Camping is that traditional log campfires are allowed, presumably to act as some kind of signal to encourage visitors from above. Wood is supplied if you let the campsite know in advance. There's nothing like a glass of wine and a few UFO stories around a roaring fire, especially at a known site of supernatural activity. If it all gets a bit scary, you can hide in the small on-site clubhouse and distract yourself with darts or pool.

Natural, rather than supernatural attractions in the area include the ancient coastal market town of Southwold with its Blue Flag beach, galleries, pier and tea shops. Nearer to the campsite is Sutton Hoo, burial ground of the Anglo-Saxon kings of East Anglia. One of the country's most significant archaeological sites, it's now managed by the National Trust. Although most of the ancient artefacts recovered from the burial chambers are displayed in the British Museum, there is a changing programme of annual exhibitions at the site itself.

Another National Trust site nearby is Orford Ness, a nature reserve centred around the largest vegetated shingle split in Europe with salt marsh and mudflat habitats attracting breeding and migrating birds. The area used to belong to the Ministry of Defence who operated a secret military testing ground here and the location is said to have played an important role in the development of the British Atomic bomb and RADAR. In an area linked with top secret military testing programmes, it's perhaps not surprising that strange, unexplained sightings have occurred. What other advanced experimental technologies were investigated at Orford Ness, we may never know.

THE UPSIDE: Campfires – and the possibility of alien encounters?

THE DOWNSIDE: There's no ignoring the hum of traffic from the A12. Shame.

THE DAMAGE: A bargain £6 per pitch per night, or £8 for an electrical hook-up. No extra charges for awnings, pets, children etc.

THE FACILITIES: Hot showers, kitchen with hot water and fridge-freezer, washing machine (charge applies), small clubhouse with TV, CD, darts and pool table (50p per game).

NEAREST DECENT PUB: There are a couple of pubs on the High Street, within staggering distance of the campsite, but a better choice is The Greyhound Inn (01728 746451) in nearby Pettistree with a good reputation for both classic and contemporary country food in a traditional pub setting. Further afield, in Bramfield, near Southwold, the Queen's Head (01986 784214) is a great little pub dishing out award-winning food including local, organic meats and a delicious seafood crumble (£10.95).

IF IT RAINS: Snape Maltings (www.snapemaltings.co.uk), is a collection of converted granaries and malthouses beside the River Alde with shops, restaurants, regular farmers' markets and a concert hall.

GETTING THERE: From the A12 take the B1078 to Wickham Market; Spring Lane is on the left.

OPEN: All year round.

IF IT'S FULL: Forest Camping (01394 450707; www.forestcamping.co.uk), in the heart of Rendlesham Forest, is a peaceful alternative.

Orchard Camping, Spring Lane, Wickham Market, Suffolk IP13 0SJ   t   01728 746170

clippesby hall

For a campsite of this size and with such extensive facilities, Clippesby Hall near Great Yarmouth in Norfolk, has managed the near-impossible. Despite its large extent, it feels friendly, non-commercial and above all, very homely.

Clippesby Hall is like its own little self-contained village. Set in the manicured grounds of a small, odd-looking manor house, the campsite has everything you could possibly want and more besides. With 100 pitches (many with electrical hook-up), an outdoor swimming pool, grass tennis courts, mini-golf, self-catering cottages, pine lodges and its own family pub, you might assume that this place is about as quiet and peaceful as a night on the hard shoulder of the A12. Well, you'd be wrong. Somehow the owner, John Lindsay, has managed to incorporate all those facilities into the grounds of his family home, while still retaining its unique character and personality. The result is an exceptionally tasteful camping park with a relaxed, family atmosphere.

The camping pitches are spread across various areas, each landscaped and spacious enough to avoid any feeling of overcrowding. Each pitch is named according to its individual character: Pine Woods is almost entirely surrounded by conifers, The Orchard has plenty of tree cover amongst the pitches while The Dell is hidden away in a quiet corner. Rabbits Grove is a favourite amongst younger campers with bunny rabbits bouncing around. These well laid-out, mid-sized clearings mean that even in busy periods, you can still find a relatively secluded space to call your own.

Clippesby Hall is in a perfect location to explore the Broads National Park, a network of rivers and lakes that forms Britain's largest protected wetland. Although the rivers are natural, the lakes are man-made, the result of 200 years of enthusiastic peat digging from the 12th century onwards. Hundreds of hectares of peat were dug up for fuel in the absence of suitable woodland in the area. However, water soon began seeping through the porous ground, causing marshes and then lakes to appear. In a centuries-old example of how human intervention can significantly change the landscape, nature has also demonstrated its resilience to adapt to a changing environment, and this collaboration of industry and nature has resulted in a stunning waterscape.

A good place to start exploring the Broads is the village of Potter Heigham, four miles north of Clippesby Hall. Several boatyards hire out a variety of vessels by the hour or day, allowing tourists to enjoy the experience of piloting their own craft. For the less adventurous, Broads Tours (01692 670711; www.broads.co.uk) at Herbert Woods Boatyard offer piloted pleasure trips complete with commentary.

When you first arrive at Clippesby Hall, don't be surprised if you're personally guided to your pitch; it's been a deliberate decision not to put large, obtrusive pitch-markers and unnecessary signs everywhere. After all, this is John's home and garden – it's been in the family for 50-odd years, and he doesn't want to ruin it by putting signs up everywhere to make it look like… well, like a campsite.

And that's the beauty of this unique place. It doesn't feel like a conventional commercial campsite. It has a far more agreeable atmosphere than that.

THE UPSIDE: Quiet and peaceful country site with good facilities.

THE DOWNSIDE: The swimming pool is too small to be much use, but is okay for a splash around.

THE DAMAGE: Prices for car, tent and two people from £13 mid-season to £19.50 high season.

THE FACILITIES: Swimming pool, grass tennis courts, kids' play area, crazy golf (£2), volleyball, football, café and shop, family pub.

NEAREST DECENT PUB: The on-site pub is called The Muskett Arms and has a limited pub grub menu. About six miles away, the Fur and Feathers (01603 720003) in Woodbastwick, is a lovely country pub with a fantastic garden for the summer. It serves decent food (mains £7–13) and Woodforde ales (including the famous Norfolk Nog) and is immediately next to the Woodforde Brewery (01603 722218) where half-hour tours are run at 7pm on Tuesdays and Thursdays.

IF IT RAINS: Glitzy Great Yarmouth, Norfolk's busiest seaside resort, with museums, amusement arcades and a casino is only 10 miles away.

GETTING THERE: From the A47 between Norwich and Great Yarmouth, take the A1064 at Acle (Caister-on-Sea road). Take the first left at Clippesby on to the B1152. Clippesby Hall is signposted.

OPEN: Apr–Oct.

IF IT'S FULL: Just a couple of miles away is the simple, country campsite of Woodside Farm (01692 670367; www.woodside-farm.co.uk), a tiny 10-pitch site in the village of Thurne with countryside views.

Clippesby Hall, Hall Lane, Clippesby, Norfolk NR29 3BL | t | 01493 367800 | w | www.clippesby.com

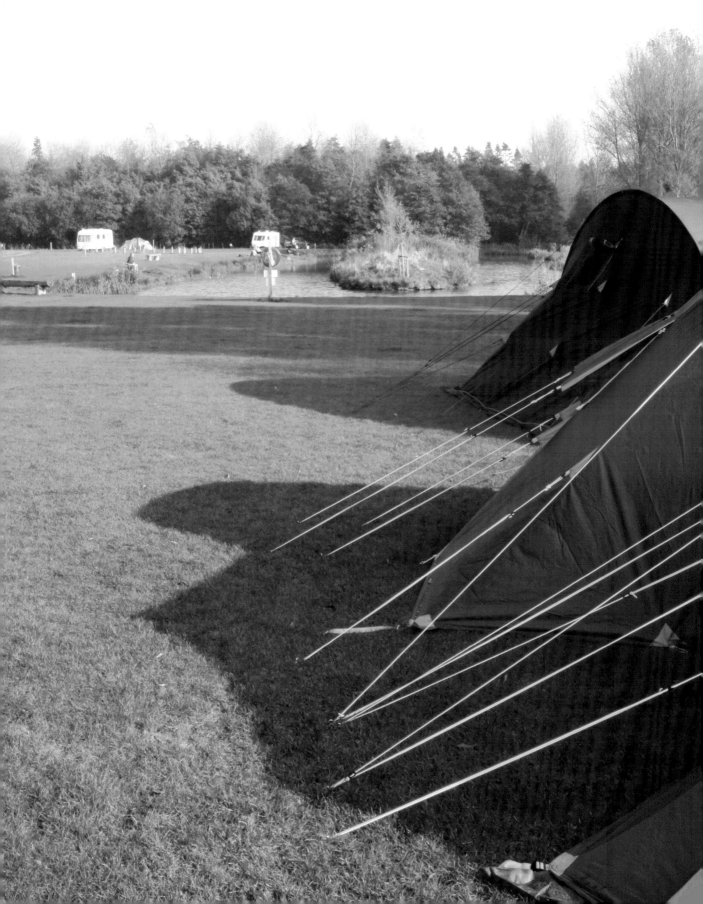

deer's glade

Contemporary bathrooms, wireless broadband internet connection, an attentive concierge service and a shuttle bus to the local pubs and other attractions. These may sound like hotel facilities, but it's all part of the service at Deer's Glade campsite between Norwich and Cromer in North Norfolk.

Set in a quiet woodland clearing, Deer's Glade is a relatively new destination that successfully combines modern innovations with old-school camping principles to create an easy, comfortable country campsite.

At first glance, it's not particularly attractive. A large, open clearing is encircled by a single-track access road, with caravan and camping pitches everywhere. But on closer inspection, it's obvious that great care and attention has been taken in creating this site. Sapling trees have been planted which, in time, will offer shade and shelter and will create a pleasant landscaped environment. The ground has been perfectly levelled and turfed to make for easy pitching. The slick, hotel-style shower facilities are housed not in ugly concrete blocks but in eco-friendly wooden buildings. A picturesque fishing lake in one corner of the site provides a natural focal point and serves to attract wildlife. The overall effect is of a high level of customer comfort, but not at the expense of nature and conservation.

Then there's the internet. The jury's out on whether broadband internet connection is an appropriate extra for a rural camping experience, but it's another indication of the lengths the owners, David and Heather, will go to for their customers – the friendliness of staff and the level of service is of the highest standard. To call it a concierge service may be slightly extravagant on our part, but organising a shuttle service to local pubs, restaurants and the station for a small fee is beyond the call of duty for most campsite owners.

From the campsite, it's possible to walk directly into the adjacent woodland, with acres of conifer-rich foliage and resident wild deer. The deer sometimes even visit the campsite, but it's easier to see them on the short walk to Gunton Park, an 800-acre park set in the grounds of an old manor house. Although the house has been converted into luxury homes, the grounds are open to the public offering lovely parkland walks and a large fishing lake stocked with carp, pike and bream.

Deer's Glade is only five miles from the Victorian seaside town of Cromer with its raised seafront promenade, long, sandy beach and end-of-the-pier shows. Cromer also has a reputation for delicious crabs, renowned for their tender, sweet flesh. Try your luck at catching them from the pier, or take the easy option and bag some nice fresh crustaceans from the fishmongers. One of the best places to enjoy this succulent seafood is at Cookies Crab Shop, a few miles west of Cromer along the coast at Salthouse. Generous fresh shellfish salads and platters are dished out at bargain prices – bring your own wine and grab a table outside in the salty sea air.

Also within easy reach are two exceptional National Trust properties. Felbrigg Hall, near Cromer, is a remarkable 17th-century house of Stuart design, with a delightful walled garden and orangery. To the south, near Aylsham, the fine Jacobean house of Blickling Hall is famed for its long gallery, fine tapestries and exquisite paintings. It's also supposedly the home of the headless ghost of Anne Boleyn.

These ancient houses hark back to an era of untold luxury and comfort. But for all their opulence and royal extravagance, even they never had wireless broadband internet access.

THE UPSIDE: Good fishing and easy walking from a peaceful campsite. Great seafood nearby.

THE DOWNSIDE: Trees yet to mature, so camping area is one big open space.

THE DAMAGE: Adult/child from £4.50/£1.50 low season to £7/£2.50 high season. Minimum three night booking on Bank Holiday weekends.

THE FACILITIES: Two brand new, spotless shower blocks with plenty of hot water and trendy limestone finishing; disabled and baby-changing facilities; on-site shop with limited supplies including tasty organic bacon and sausages; kids'

play area; fishing available on site (£4.40) or next door at Gunton Hall (£4.50; no night fishing).

NEAREST DECENT PUB: The Alby Horse Shoes Inn (01263 761378) back on the main road is a very traditional pub untouched by modernity, with four real ales and a menu of £6–10 meals. If you're exploring the coast, the Red Lion Inn (01263 825408) in Upper Sheringham is worth making a stop at, a 300-year-old flint pub with a Snug Bar and a menu featuring locally caught fish.

IF IT RAINS: Felbrigg Hall (open Sat–Wed) and Blickling Hall (Wed–Sun) are within a few miles; Cromer and Sheringham on the coast are well worth a visit; or check to see if Norwich FC (www.canaries.co.uk) are playing at home.

GETTING THERE: From Norwich, take the A140 towards Cromer. Five miles beyond Aylsham, turn right towards Suffield Green, signposted White Post Road. The site is half a mile on the right.

OPEN: All year round.

IF IT'S FULL: Clippesby Hall (p154) and Pinewoods (p166) are both within easy reach.

Deer's Glade, White Post Road, Hanworth, Norwich, Norfolk NR11 7HN | t | 01263 768633 | w | www.deersglade.co.uk

pinewoods

Beach huts are a great British tradition. Maybe it's the fact that we can never trust the weather enough to be able to spend a whole day on the beach without shelter. Or maybe it's because most of us can't afford a waterside home. Either way, these quirky little beach boxes have become an endearing symbol of the British seaside.

In recent years, beach huts have also become the sought-after alternative to a second home. In some parts of the country, these little wooden wonders have been known to change hands for more than £200,000. All that money and you're not even allowed to sleep in your own property – council regulations prohibit overnight stays. The alternative to purchasing your own beach hut is a trip to Pinewoods campsite at Wells-next-the-Sea on the north Norfolk coast, where beach huts can be rented by the day or by the week, complete with deckchairs and windbreaks.

Pinewoods isn't a typical *Cool Camping* campsite. It's a big, commercial site, home to hundreds of unattractive static caravans. They don't even treat their tent campers particularly well, squeezing them into a modest-sized camping area by the boating lake, which tends to flood in heavy rain.

In summer, however, they open up the Horse Paddock, a larger field where you can pick your own pitch amongst the shelter of the tall grass and spread out a bit. It's quite a trek from here to the main amenities blocks, although portaloos and running water are on hand.

Despite treating canvas campers as second-class citizens, the on-site facilities at Pinewoods are good. There's a safe and extensive children's play area and plenty of showers, toilets and washing-up facilities. More importantly, a beachside campsite with beach huts for hire is a very rare thing.

Wells beach can be found at the northern end of the campsite, through some tall pine trees and over a vegetation-covered sand dune. If you arrive here at high tide, you might be unimpressed; a long row of assorted beach huts hugs the sandbank with just a few metres of beach at their feet. However, as the tide recedes, more and more of the beach is revealed until low tide, when a huge expanse of golden sand spreads out as far as the eye can see. It's perfect for sandcastle-making, kite-flying, dog-walking and swimming. It also makes a great view from the terrace of your rented beach hut,

perhaps while enjoying a romantic barbecue dinner for two.

Pinewoods is a perfect base from which to explore the north Norfolk coast, a good stretch of which is within walking or cycling distance. A walk westwards along the Norfolk Coast Path takes you through Holkham Nature Reserve, with miles of dunes and sand-spits, conifer woods and intricate, changing tidal landscapes. Bikes can be hired from Pinewoods for an idyllic cycle through country lanes, to appealing villages such as Burnham Deepdale and Burnham Market, complete with delicious local delis and award-winning gastropubs.

Holkham Hall is the local manor house, a Palladian-style mansion that is still a family home to the Earl of Leicester and the Coke family, owners of much of this area including Pinewoods campsite. Many of the state rooms are open to the public including the highly imposing Marble Hall, with 50-foot ceilings and intricate designs. The Deer Park and grounds are also open to walkers and cyclists.

You can't fail to be impressed by Holkham Hall, an immaculately maintained estate. But the one thing it lacks is the direct sea view. You'll need a beach hut for that. Just as well the Coke family own those too.

THE UPSIDE: Beach huts, sand dunes, miles of sandy beaches, Norfolk Coast Path.

THE DOWNSIDE: Big, commercial site catering mainly for static holiday homes.

THE DAMAGE: Tents £9–£14 per night; motorhomes and caravans from £12–£25. Beach huts from £8 per day in low season to £21 during midsummer.

THE FACILITIES: Several shower blocks with plenty of showers, toilets and washing-up sinks, kids' playground, well-stocked mini-market, café, boating lake with canoes and rowing boats for hire, trampolines, crazy golf, pool room, bike hire.

NEAREST DECENT PUB: For a local pint and good-value bar food, The Globe Inn (01328 710206) in Wells is the best bet. Slightly further afield are two exceptional gastropubs. The Victoria (01328 713230) at the entrance to Holkham Hall has a changing restaurant menu featuring local ingredients. In Burnham Market, The Hoste Arms (01328 738777) continues to win accolades for its imaginative menu and well-priced wines.

IF IT RAINS: Holkham Hall is two miles away, while the interesting seaside town of Cromer (p164) is the same distance in the other direction. If the weather gets really bad, you might be tempted to book yourself into the fantastic rooms at The Victoria or The Hoste Arms.

GETTING THERE: Wells-next-the-Sea is 30 miles northwest of Norwich as the crow flies. From the A149 coast road, follow the signs to Wells and then to the beach. Pinewoods is almost at the end of Beach Road on the left.

OPEN: Mar–Nov.

IF IT'S FULL: For a smaller campsite with a totally different vibe, check out High Sand Creek (01328 830119) at Stiffkey. No beach huts, bells or whistles, it's a simple site on the Norfolk Coast Path, overlooking the salt marsh and sea.

Pinewoods, Beach Road, Wells-next-the-Sea, Norfolk NR23 1DR | t | 01328 710439 | w | www.pinewoods.co.uk

longnor wood

In the southern 'White Peak' area of the Peak District, surrounded by shallow hills, sits the village of Longnor. It's an idyllic place with a cobbled market square, pretty cottages fashioned from local stone and a thriving industry in clockmaking. The slow-paced, old-world ambiance is enhanced by the gentle melody of peeling church bells. An inscription above the old market hall lists the tariffs for trading here – as of 1873.

It's the sort of place that city dwellers visit for a weekend and immediately decide they'd like to move to. Most don't, of course, but Paul and Lindsey Hedges did. Already keen campers and on the lookout for a lifestyle change from their careers in bricklaying and banking, they came across Longnor Wood, a campsite on the outskirts of the village. Its current owners were moving on and it was up for sale. Within a few short months, they'd snapped it up, ditched their jobs and moved their lives from urban Bristol to rural Derbyshire.

They then set about creating the sort of campsite they would want to stay in. It was already an adults-only site when they took it over and the absence of kids running around seemed fitting for such a peaceful location amongst the dales. So the rule remained. They set aside some of the 20 acres for wildlife, planted more trees to screen the tents from the surrounding hills and opted for as spacious pitches as they could accommodate.

The result is a tranquil campsite that maximises the great location and minimises its environmental impact. Three small, gently sloping fields are surrounded by woodland and farmland, offering tantalising glimpses of the Peak National Park. All the essential facilities are here, but Paul and Lindsey have made a conscious decision not to pander to the extravagant needs of satellite-TV campers. They've avoided cash-generating super-pitches and electricity in the camping fields, not just for environmental reasons but because it goes against the spirit of camping. With stunning countryside all around, why would anyone want to sit inside and watch TV?

Extra touches include a French-style boules court, a 9-hole putting green and badminton. But Paul and Lindsey are keen to stress that the campsite's major attractions are not on the site at all, but all around it.

The market town of Buxton, home to a natural warm-water spring discovered by the Romans, is only six miles away. It's sometimes known as the Bath of the north – given the similarity to its better-visited southern cousin – and not just for its spa credentials. Grand Georgian and Victorian architecture dominates in its historic core, where a sweeping curve of houses is reminiscent of the famous Bath Royal Crescent. The lovingly restored Opera House here is well worth a visit; tours are available on Saturday mornings at 11am, or if you're visiting during the July Opera Festival, you might be lucky enough to get a ticket for a performance. Buxton is also the place to be on Tuesdays and Saturdays when Market Place comes alive with a plethora of stalls, friendly, vocal stallholders and browsing shoppers. This is also the centre for eating and drinking in Buxton, with numerous little cafés and restaurants.

Longnor Wood is an ideal base for walking amongst the rugged scenery of the Peak District. Easily-followed paths criss-cross the nearby Upper Dove and Manifold Valleys with a variety of routes for all abilities. The distinguished walks and views around here are quite something, with Dove Ridge, in particular, the place to head to for a stunning outlook and gentle inspiration. Who knows, you might even end up wanting to move here.

THE UPSIDE: Well-run campsite with dale views – and no kids!

THE DOWNSIDE: Can get busy in summer and on Bank Holidays.

THE DAMAGE: Tent and up to two people £12.50, standard caravan/motorhome pitch £14.50, extra person £3.

THE FACILITIES: Heated toilet block, hot showers, shop, laundry room, boules, badminton, putting.

NEAREST DECENT PUB: There are a few decent pubs in Longnor, but a mile further on is the outstanding Packhorse Inn (01298 83618) in Crowdecote, a beautiful old limestone pub with a reputation for good food and tasty ales. It'll take just over half an hour to walk there, quite possibly longer to walk back.

IF IT RAINS: Buxton has everything you need to make a rainy weekend fun. Tour the Opera House (0845 1272190) or enjoy cream teas in Edwardian style at Hargreaves Coffee Shop (01298 23083).

GETTING THERE: Longnor is six miles southeast of Buxton. From Longnor, follow the brown caravan signs along the Longnor-Leek road for one mile.

OPEN: Mar–Oct.

IF IT'S FULL: Just off the A6 at Blackwell-in-the-Peak is Cottage Farm Caravan Park (01298 85330), a compact site with Peak views from the tent pitches, which are in a separate field from the caravans.

Longnor Wood Caravan and Camping Park, Longnor, Nr Buxton, Derbyshire SK17 0NG

| t | 01298 83648 | w | www.longnorwood.co.uk |

fieldhead

Question: What's the busiest National Park in Europe and the second busiest in the world after Mount Fuji? Unexpected answer: The Peak District in England's Midlands.

The Peak District's surprising popularity may be partially attributed to its proximity to the densely-populated conurbations of Sheffield, Manchester and Derby, but that's not the full story. It's a unique and striking wilderness with a rare diversity of landscapes created by two completely different geological foundations. The Dark Peak to the north spreads across coarse sandstone terrain and is notorious for peaty bogs and tall cliffs. The gentler White Peak to the south sits on a foundation of limestone and is characterised by green fields and rolling hills. Roughly where the two areas meet is Fieldhead campsite in Edale, surrounded by green countryside and with direct views across this distinctive landscape. Quite simply, it's a rambler's paradise in the heart of some of the best walking country in England.

The campsite is made up of five intimately-sized fields set at varying levels on a riverside hillock with plenty of shelter provided by fences and hedges. There are no marked pitches, so pick an area that suits

you – our favourite was in the shade of the trees down by the stream, the running water providing an appropriate soundtrack. It's an exceptionally small campsite, so nowhere is really far from the amenities block, a clean and regularly maintained shed-like structure in a convenient central position.

The quiet, countryside feel of Fieldhead is enhanced by the fact that cars cannot be driven onto the site. There's a car park at the entrance (don't forget to reserve a space when booking your pitch) and because it's such a small site, it's not far to lug your gear from the car, wherever you choose to pitch. Many people camping here don't have a car at all, as it's within walking distance of Edale train station and is on some major long-distance walking thoroughfares.

The fact that there is a Visitor Centre and Ranger's Office on site is an added bonus, as you'll find all the information you need to make the most of your visit. By the time you read this, it will have been redeveloped and reopened as the Moors for the Future Centre, a showcase for the preservation and conservation of the moors, with the same helpful staff, bundles of local information and handy walking guides. Most of the book-guided treks start from this Visitor

Centre, so it's ideal. The proximity to the station also means that you can plan a walk to other stations along the line and return easily to the campsite.

Fieldhead is a popular launch pad for the Pennine Way, an epic 270-mile path that starts in Edale and heads north along the Pennine Ridge, through the Yorkshire Dales and Northumberland, finishing up at the Scottish Borders. It's one of England's great walks across challenging and changing terrain. You might not want to attempt the whole path, but the first leg, from Edale to Cowden is a good taster, a 16-mile trek taking in some fine Peak District scenery.

An alternative local walk is the Edale Horseshoe, a testing and strenuous circuit that follows the skyline around the edge of the valley, depositing the tired walker back in Edale some 18 miles later. There are plenty of other walks and rambles for all levels; many of the shorter hops deliver just as memorable scenery as some of the longer trails.

Whether you're following the path well trod across the Pennines or discovering the lesser-trampled treasures of Edale, Fieldhead, a perfect base camp, will get you off on the right foot.

THE UPSIDE: Fantastic walking from this miniature campsite.

THE DOWNSIDE: The trains can be noisy during the night. Also, the insects are quite friendly, especially by the river at dusk. Take repellent.

THE DAMAGE: Tents only, no caravans or motorhomes. Adults £3.50–4.50, children £2.50–3, parking £1.50–2.

THE FACILITIES: Hot showers are 20p, so bring some coins! Disabled facilities and laundry services available. No shop on site – there's a general stores in town, but don't rely on it, bring everything you need.

NEAREST DECENT PUB: The Ramblers Inn (01433 670268) in Edale is a well-presented renovation of an old pub, serving real ales and reasonable food. You can survey the scenery from the beer garden. Folk music nights on occasional Wednesdays through the summer can be great fun.

IF IT RAINS: The local settlement of Castleton is home to several dramatic caves, including Peak Cavern (01433 620512) and Speedwell Cavern (01433 620512), both of which offer worthwhile guided tours. The latter features an underground lake reached by boat – not for the claustrophobic.

GETTING THERE: Edale is about 10 miles northeast of Buxton. Follow the signs for Edale from the A265. As you approach the village, Fieldhead is on the right just after the Ramblers Inn.

OPEN: All year round.

IF IT'S FULL: Coopers Campsite (01433 670372; www.edale-valley.co.uk/coopers) is a larger site on the same road which takes caravans and motorhomes as well as tents.

Fieldhead Campsite, Edale, Hope Valley, Derbyshire S33 7ZA | t | 01433 670386 | w | www.fieldhead-campsite.co.uk

upper booth farm

What can you do when hundreds of people – all total strangers – insist on walking through your garden? Thousands of them, in fact. Tramping around with big muddy boots and walking sticks, chattering away excitedly, the inconsiderate wretches.

Of course, this isn't your bog-standard garden. This is 970 acres of prime Derbyshire livestock farmland in one of the most renowned valleys in the Peak District. It's also the home and garden of Robert and Sarah Helliwell, National Trust tenants and life-long farmers. But for the transient visitors, it's something else entirely – it's the main thoroughfare of the Pennine Way.

The Pennine Way is Britain's most popular footpath. It's estimated that around 250,000 walkers use the section in the Peak District every year. Not all of them walk the entire path, but around 10,000 do. That's a lot of people walking through Upper Booth Farm each year. It doesn't seem to bother Robert and Sarah too much; they're used to the steady and varied stream of hikers, everyone from sprightly newcomers, breaking themselves in on the first stretch that starts just down the road in Edale village, to tired and aching long-distance walkers completing the path in the other direction. As the first port of call after the Kinder Scout Plateau, walkers are always stopping here in need of plasters, refreshments or emergency services, all tirelessly organised by Upper Booth's custodians when the need arises. But the most useful service provided by Robert and Sarah is a handy place to crash for the night, at their scenic campsite.

The backdrop to the two camping fields at Upper Booth is pretty spectacular, with tight folds of low Pennine hills dominating the skyline. The trickle and tumble of spindly Crowden Brook can be heard as it washes down from the Kinder Scout plateau, cutting a deep channel in the land to one side of the main camping field. Like the best countryside campsites, it's difficult to see where the site ends and the open landscape of the Peaks begins: it all seems to merge into one continuous topography.

The campsite stretches across two fields at the other side of the farmhouse to where the Pennine walkers pass. The first, smaller field is flat, sheltered and near to the facilities. The second field is a larger, undulating area of grass, open to the Peak

District views, with a line of tall trees marking one side of the campsite and Cowden Brook marking the other. The amenities are on the rustic side: a shower a-piece for men and women in a draughty old stone barn. They do need upgrading, but because this is National Trust land, permission to build new facilities is slow to obtain.

Walkers can also make use of a handy camping barn. The traditional stone structure used to house livestock, but it now has a wooden sleeping platform and

tables and chairs for up to 12 weary Pennine walkers who don't have the strength or energy to put up a tent.

The farm itself is innovative and environmentally friendly and has been selected as a demonstration farm due to the sustainable and integrated farming techniques used here. Robert's objective is to produce safe, healthy food while also respecting the environment, and he's won awards for his achievements. If there was an award for services to walkers, they'd get that too.

THE UPSIDE: Peak District views all around from this prime walkers' site.

THE DOWNSIDE: The facilities are very basic and need updating.

THE DAMAGE: Camping £3 per person; £1 per car; £5 per person in the camping barn. No caravans allowed on site.

THE FACILITIES: Flush toilets, hot showers, washing-up facilities, camping barn. There's no shop, but you might get a few essentials like milk, eggs, bread, confectionery, locally made ice

creams, barbecues and prime farm meat if you knock on the farmhouse door.

NEAREST DECENT PUB: From the campsite, it's a half-hour walk along the first (or last) stretch of the Pennine Way to the 'official' start/end point of the path at The Old Nag's Head pub (01433 670291) in Edale village. This historic inn has great potential, but until they sort out the surly staff, tacky décor and indifferent food, you may prefer The Rambler's Inn (see p178) down the road.

IF IT RAINS: See page 178 for details of the caves at Castleton.

GETTING THERE: Upper Booth Farm is a mile from Edale village in the Hope valley, about 10 miles northeast of Buxton. Follow the signs for Edale from the A625, look out for the signpost to Upper Booth a mile west of the turning for Edale village and station. Follow the road all the way to the end.

OPEN: All year; winter camping by prior arrangement.

IF IT'S FULL: Fieldhead campsite (p176) is just down the road.

Upper Booth Farm, Upper Booth, nr Edale, Hope Valley, Derbyshire S33 7ZJ

| | t | 01433 670250 | w | www.upperboothcamping.co.uk |

jerusalem farm

Camping is all about getting closer to nature, so what better place to camp than in a nature reserve. Jerusalem Farm local nature reserve in the picturesque Luddenden Valley, near Halifax, couldn't be better placed.

Luddenden is a steep and narrow valley, an almost-hidden gorge deep in the heart of Pennine Yorkshire. Luddenden Beck, long exploited by local mills for its fast-flowing waters, runs along its base and it is by the banks of this brook that Jerusalem Farm is sited. As a nature reserve, it's a pristine slice of Pennine perfection, with untouched woods on the surrounding slopes, steep valley walls protecting the area from development and the constant chirping of birdsong the only challenge to the noise of the gushing river. As at an increasing number of peaceful campsites, vehicles aren't permitted; cars are parked by reception at the top of the valley slope and equipment must be carried down to the camping fields.

The Luddenden and adjacent Calder Valleys are rich in industrial heritage. The old mill towns of Hebden Bridge, Todmorden and Sowerby Bridge had their heyday during the 19th-century textile boom as river-powered looms replaced traditional hand looms. These villages have not changed significantly since before the Industrial Revolution and all retain their mill houses and much of their character. In Hebden Bridge, however, while the buildings remain true to the past, the atmosphere is decidedly New Age. The town is now the self-styled 'alternative' capital of the north of England, known for a vibrant arts scene, an eclectic vibe and one of the largest gay and lesbian communities north of Soho. It has also been hailed as one of the least cloned towns in England, standing firm against the invasion of dreary chain stores and supermarkets to retain a highly individual, independent character where good-quality, locally-produced goods are favoured. Family butchers, traditional bakers and well-stocked delicatessens share the high street with quirky coffee shops, organic restaurants and galleries, with not a Woollies in sight.

As well as an eclectic resident community, Hebden Bridge sees a steady stream of tourists attracted by local links to Ted Hughes (born near here), Sylvia Plath (buried near here), and the Bronte sisters (lived in nearby Haworth). Visitors are also drawn by the exceptional hill-walking to be found in this region, which no doubt served as inspiration to these literary greats. The Pennine Way (see p181) dissects this area

north to south, and The Calderdale Way, a circular 50-mile walk stretching from Todmorden through Hebden Bridge, Halifax and Sowerby Bridge, follows old packhorse routes and moorland paths through this untouched scenery. You're likely to spot plenty of wildlife on a stroll: much of this area is protected countryside and an important breeding and nesting area for distinctive birds including the curvy-beaked curlew and the splendid, crested lapwing. You'll also see red grouse hopping around wherever there's an abundance of heather. If all this is just too much nature and wildlife, the mini-metropolis of Halifax can give you an urban fix, with browsing to be had at Piece Hall, a historic marketplace for

textiles and now home to speciality shops, boutiques and weekend markets. Bars and restaurants are also thriving here, although Hebden Bridge, and to a lesser extent Sowerby Bridge, are gaining a reputation for their gastronomy.

Pennine Yorkshire is undoubtedly a jewel in England's landscape, yet it's often overlooked as a destination, with the substantial attractions of the Lake District and both coasts within an easy drive. But take the time to visit, to scratch beneath the surface, and you'll find yourself strongly attracted to this wild, understated landscape. The call of nature, so to speak.

THE UPSIDE: A car-free riverside campsite at the foot of a small valley.

THE DOWNSIDE: Basic facilities, only one shower, too many midges, take repellent.

THE DAMAGE: Adults £5, children £3. Tents only; no caravans or motorhomes. No unaccompanied under-18s.

THE FACILITIES: Toilets, shower, children's play area, picnic tables.

NEAREST DECENT PUB: There's a great little pub nearby named the Cat-I'th-Well (01422 244841)

which sells Timothy Taylor's bitter and, curiously for a pub, free range eggs, although there's no suggestion you should drink them together as some strange new cocktail. It's a half-hour walk or 10-minute drive.

IF IT RAINS: Hebden Bridge and Sowerby Bridge both have various culinary and cultural diversions. Eureka Museum for Children (01422 330069; www.eureka.org.uk) in Halifax can help keep the little ones entertained. Or for something totally different, try the Halifax Ski & Snowboard Centre (01422 340760).

GETTING THERE: From the A646 at Luddenden Foot turn up Luddenden Lane at the restaurant. After one-and-a-half miles, turn right towards Booth. Go through the village and after the sharp left-hand bend, Jerusalem Lane is 20 metres on the left. Look out for the campsite on the right.

OPEN: Easter–Sep.

IF IT'S FULL: Rough Hey Wood Campsite (01422 834586) in Stansfield Mill Lane, Triangle, occupies a lovely woodland setting, just a couple of miles south of Jerusalem Farm.

Jerusalem Farm, Jerusalem Lane, Booth, Halifax, West Yorkshire HX2 6XB   t | 01422 883246   f | 01422 393276

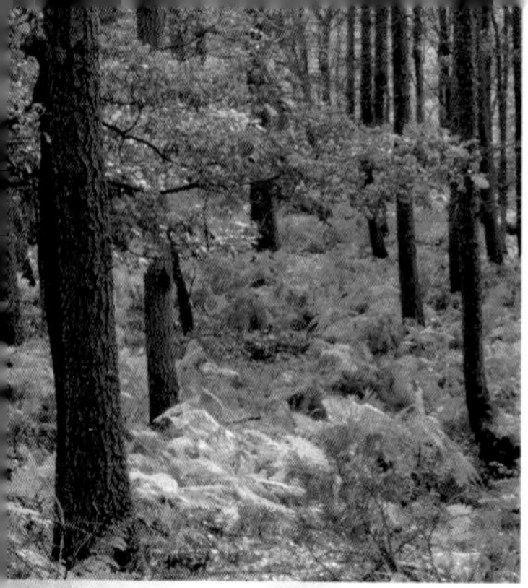

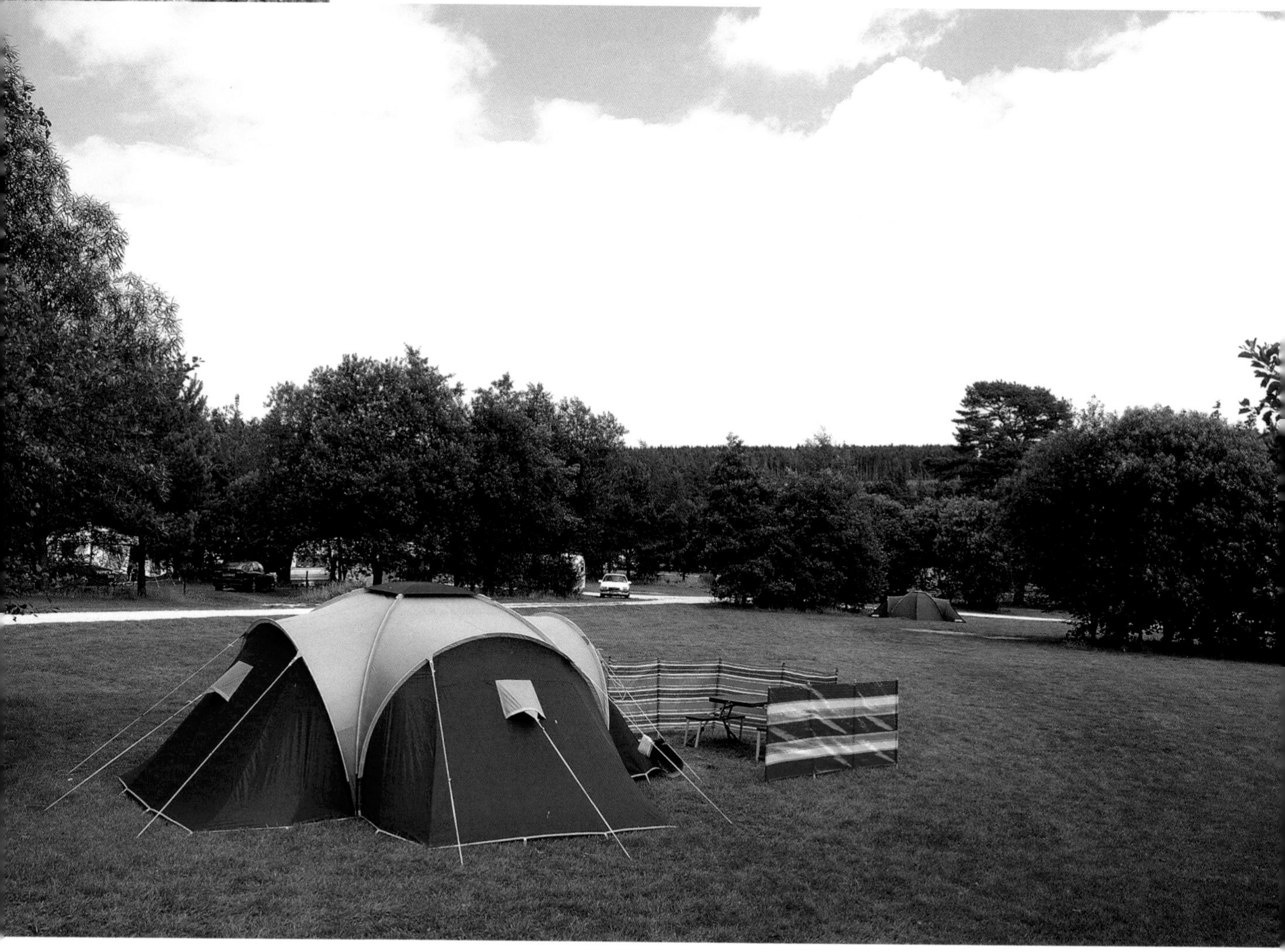

spiers house

Spiers House Campsite is one of the best campsites owned and run by the Forestry Commission. It's situated in the heart of Cropton Forest about 20 miles west of Scarborough in the North Yorks Moors National Park. Those are the facts. The facts don't tell you what an amazing area this is for a varied and active holiday.

The main thing to remember before setting off for Spiers House is to pack a mountain bike. And if you've got children lurking in the back of the car, make sure they haven't forgotten theirs either. What you find when you turn off the public highway towards Spiers House, is a long winding driveway that takes you deep into the forest, and goes nowhere else. The setting of this medium-sized campsite is undeniably pretty, with all the feeling of a remote, magical woodland, but without the trees being too overpowering or blocking out the sun. All around is miles of hassle-free, traffic-free (but not necessarily effort-free!) cycling within Cropton Forest. You can set the little darlings free and know that no vehicular harm will befall them.

If mundane matters such as the standard of site facilities bother you, then worry not about Spiers House as we found this to be the most efficiently run Forestry Commission site yet, with excellent facilities and a very handy shop – a necessity for a campsite so remotely situated.

Whilst the biking is exceptional around here, there is one standard tourist attraction which should be considered for a day out in conjunction with the bike. This is the North Yorkshire Moors Steam Railway, which puffs and chugs its way between Pickering and Grosmont, a complete nostalgia overload. Non-bikers can drive down to Pickering to pick up the train, whilst those on two wheels can pedal over to Levisham Station and lock up the bikes before boarding the train northwards. Another great cycling day out, combined with some sightseeing, is to start on the cycle tracks, then follow the country lanes over to the sweet little village of Goathland, which has been swallowed almost whole by TV 'Heartbeat' hysteria.

Should the legs need a break, then Scarborough is only about 20 miles away to the east, with a great deal of charm about the place and some quietly dramatic scenery surrounding the seafront amusement arcades.

Still within day-out range is the lovely, quirky little town of Whitby, where they manage to combine the various qualities and drawbacks of fishing port, historical town and seaside resort with seamless, intriguing ease. Other coastal attractions are the irresistible villages of Robin Hood's Bay (p195) and beautiful little Staithes, which should be on everybody's must-see list.

But the main event has to be the biking, and up on the moors above Rosedale, in the lower reaches of which Spiers House is situated, is an off-road biking route which cannot be bettered anywhere in Britain. It's a hard day's cycling for us mortals, but the circuit of Farndale, starting at Bank Top above Rosedale Abbey is superb. Once the bike has been pushed or pedalled up to Bank Top, the track, which largely follows a slice of countryside that was previously a railway, stays above the thousand-foot contour for nearly 15 miles. The cycle back, through Hutton Le Hole, certainly tests the legs, but such is the stuff of true adventure, of which there are plentiful opportunities from Spiers House.

THE UPSIDE: Fantastic off-road biking opportunities all around. Beautifully situated for a tranquil, hassle-free holiday.

THE DOWNSIDE: A long way from the shops – and beware of the midges!

THE DAMAGE: Tent and two people £7.90–£14.70 per night, extra people (over five years) additional £2.20 each.

THE FACILITIES: Very good, with toilets, hot showers, disabled facilities, laundry, washing-up sinks and children's play area. On-site shop sells food, maps, gas refills and camping accessories.

NEAREST DECENT PUB: No pub for miles!

IF IT RAINS: Plenty on offer around here. The North Yorkshire Moors Railway (01751 472508; www.northyorkshiremoorsrailway.com) is a lovely day out. The bright lights of Scarborough are also within easy reach. Castle Howard (01653 648444; www.castlehoward.co.uk) is impressive and worthwhile; for non-cyclists there is Dalby Forest Drive (01751 472771; www.forestry.gov.uk/dalbyforest). For something different, try a visit to the Cropton Brewery (01751 417330; www.croptonbrewery.com).

GETTING THERE: From the A170 (Thirsk to Scarborough) two miles before Pickering, at the village of Wrelton, take the minor road signed to Rosedale Abbey, then a mile beyond Cropton, turn right into the forest, signposted for the site.

OPEN: Apr–Sep.

IF IT'S FULL: Other recommended campsites within easy reach are Rosedale Camping Park at Rosedale Abbey (01751 417272) and Wayside Caravan and Camping Park at Wrelton (01751 472608).

Spiers House Campsite, Cropton Forest, Cropton, Pickering, North Yorkshire YO18 8ES

| t | 01751 417591 | w | www.forestholidays.co.uk |

hooks house farm

Robin Hood's Bay, near Whitby in North Yorkshire, is an area steeped in romance and intrigue. Its very name is a mystery: there's nothing to link this place with the infamous hero of Sherwood Forest, but the name stands as an inexplicable suggestion of some legendary past.

What's certain is that this was smuggler country. Throughout the 18th century, locals crippled by high taxes turned to smuggling to make money, receiving tobacco, brandy, rum and silk from Holland and France. Gangs of smugglers used a network of underground passages and secret tunnels to deliver the stash inland, making a tidy profit in the process.

Even now, the charming town of Robin Hood's Bay, also known locally as Bay Town, or simply Bay, has the feel of an age-old smugglers' den, with unfeasibly narrow streets and tight passageways. Ancient fishermen's cottages cling to a near-vertical slope as the cliff drops down to a little fishing harbour at the water's edge. In addition to the older part of town on the side of the cliff, there's a newer enclave on the flat ground at the top. The well-ordered Victorian mansions are a world apart from the cobbled jumble below.

It has to be said, Robin Hood's Bay, although picturesque, doesn't have a 'lie-on-the-sand' beach. The ground at the foot of the bay is dark and rocky, more suitable for bracing walks, exploring rock pools and fossil-hunting than sunbathing. But the wide sweep of bay is stunning, and a great vantage point from which to enjoy this vista is at Hooks House Farm campsite on the hill above the town.

Hooks House Farm is a friendly, family-run campsite occupying a grassy field that slopes gently down towards the bay. The first-rate views really make this site: from here you can watch the tide wash in and out over the whole sweep of the bay and beyond. The campsite vibe is peaceful, relaxed and low-key, with no organised entertainment and no long list of rules and regulations to adhere to. The site is adjacent to a road, but as the road isn't inundated with vehicles you're more likely to be bothered by sheep bleating in the nearby fields than by traffic noise.

The owners, Jill and Gordon Halder, are famously attentive, ensuring that all facilities are kept suitably clean and that all visitors have everything they need. The facilities are adequate rather than

exceptional, with two showers in each of the prefab amenities blocks, although there are plans to double this capacity. Extra services include stables for hire on this working farm, so you can even bring your horse on holiday.

With the Yorkshire Moors within striking distance, the countryside is perfect for walking and cycling as well as horse riding. The disused railway line that runs though here on its way from Scarborough to Whitby has been transformed into a popular walking and cycling path, and it forms part of the wittily-named Moor to Sea cycle path, a long-distance route that provides up to four days of cycling. Robin Hood's Bay also marks the eastern end of the classic Coast to Coast Walk from St Bees Head, a superb two-week walk taking in three National Parks: The Lake District, The Yorkshire Dales and the North Yorkshire Moors.

If it's shorter walks you're after, try the half-mile stretch along a country path to Robin Hood's Bay village and its selection of five pubs, all great venues for discussing the demise of smuggling as a lucrative career, the possibility of finding fossils on the beach and for speculating how Robin Hood's Bay might have found its name.

THE UPSIDE: Panoramic bay views and easy walks.
THE DOWNSIDE: Light sleepers might be affected by slight traffic and sheep noise.
THE DAMAGE: From £4 per adult, £2 per child, £2 extra for electrical hook-up.
THE FACILITIES: Showers, toilets, use of electric kettle, stables, electrical hook-ups.

NEAREST DECENT PUB: Of the five pubs in town, our favourite is The Dolphin (01947 880337) for its cosy old-world smugglers' feel, but The Bay Hotel (01947 880278), right down by the quayside, has sea views.
IF IT RAINS: The busy fishing harbour of Whitby, some five miles to the north, deserves investigation. Attractions include Whitby Abbey and the Captain Cook Museum (01947 601900).

GETTING THERE: Heading south from Whitby on the A171, take the B1447 signposted to Robin Hood's Bay. Hooks House Farm is on the right, a half mile before the village.
OPEN: All year.
IF IT'S FULL: More sea views can be had from Bay Ness Farm (www.baynessfarm.co.uk) in a rural location adjacent to the North Yorks 4x4 Off-Road Centre. They only accept campers who have booked in advance via the internet.

Hooks House Farm, Whitby Road, Robin Hood's Bay, North Yorkshire YO22 4PE

| | t | 01947 880283 | w | www.hookshousefarm.co.uk |

gibraltar farm, morecambe bay

Morecambe Bay is a big landscape in little old England. The sweeping bay stretches for miles along the northwest coast, with an extended shoreline taking in a multitude of villages and towns from Fleetwood, just north of Blackpool, past the town of Morecambe, to Barrow-in-Furness on the Cumbrian coast, a road trip of around 70 miles. At low tide, the water in the bay completely disappears, to be replaced by acres of seemingly endless inter-tidal mudflats and sandflats that look like they belong to another planet entirely. Behind the bay, the mountain peaks of the Lake District add drama to the skyline.

This big landscape is, in turns, both beautiful and dangerous. On a hot Bank Holiday with the tide out and children playing in the golden sand, it's an innocent summer delight. But if an occasional shroud of sea mist seems ominous and foreboding, it's because the sand holds hidden dangers. Many a cockle-picker or sand-walking traveller from the far shore have been trapped by the fast-rising tide, and not all have survived to tell the tale. However, fear not – the reality is that with the smallest amount of common sense, you can easily avoid any danger and enjoy the sands.

One of the best places from which to enjoy the sands is at Gibraltar Farm campsite near Silverdale. Excuse the entrance to the campsite, where hundreds of old tyres are piled up in one corner (it's a working farm, so we'll let them off) and keep going to the camping area at the back of the farm. The access road takes you down through a lovely, terraced caravan field commanding glorious views across the bay. At the foot of this slope is a flatter area for motorhomes and caravans, surrounded by dry-stone walls and tall trees. This is where the warden and the facilities block can be found. Beyond the trees is the tent field, a large grassy area set around a rocky protrusion where rope swings have been tied to the trees. You may well find some shy sheep grazing here, quite happy to share the field with the campers, provided they don't start munching on the grass. The waters of Morecambe Bay can be seen just beyond the low wall.

Less than a mile away from the campsite is the peninsula of Jenny Brown's Point, a popular viewpoint and birdwatching spot overlooking the bay. Morecambe Bay is recognised as one of the most important sites for birdlife in the UK, as the sands are

full of crustaceans, shellfish and worms, providing a tasty feast for visiting birds. A huge range of birds can be seen here at any time of year, including pink-footed geese, oystercatcher, bittern and the odd kestrel. The centre of birdwatching activity is at nearby Leighton Moss where an RSPB reserve offers access to coastal lagoons, nature trials, hides and a Visitor Centre.

Aside from its bird population, Morecambe is famous for two other reasons. The first is Eric Morecambe, the classic English comedian, and one half of Morecambe and Wise. He was born and raised in the town and there's a statue of him in typical prancing pose on the seafront to commemorate the fact. The second is cockle-picking, for which conditions on the vast expanse of sand are perfect. Cockle-pickers can make up to £500 a day, so it's big business, although tourists can also have fun picking for themselves. Just be sure to take advice about the tides, which can be fast and deadly. If in any doubt, leave it to the professionals. It certainly pays to be wise in Morecambe.

THE UPSIDE: Farm camping with bay views.

THE DOWNSIDE: The warden needs to stamp down on late-night party noise.

THE DAMAGE: Tent with one/two/four people is £5/8/10; caravan without/with electric hook-up is £9/10. No charge for cars or awnings.

THE FACILITIES: Flush toilets, washing-up facilities, electric hook-ups; only one male and one female shower, so expect to queue. Ice creams and drinks are available from the warden. Supplies are available in nearby Silverdale, but a better choice of shops including a great butchers (Poteau & Son Continental Butchers; 01524 761217) and a post office can be found at Arnside.

NEAREST DECENT PUB: The Silverdale Hotel (01524 701206) in the village is less than a mile away, but aside from a pleasant beer garden, isn't very inspiring. There are some better pubs in Arnside, about three miles away, where The Albion (01524 761226) has a waterside beer garden, real ales and an interesting menu.

IF IT RAINS: The RSPB reserve at Leighton Moss is open from 9am–dusk (free to RSPB members; adults £4; children £1). Almost opposite the campsite is the Wolfhouse Gallery (01524 701405), displaying paintings, ceramics and jewelry. There is also a good café serving light lunches, tea and cakes.

GETTING THERE: Silverdale is about 11 miles southwest of Kendal. From the A6, take the B5282 to Arnside, then follow the signs to Silverdale. Go through the village, then follow Hollins Lane for less than a mile; as the road turns sharply to the left, Gibraltar Farm is on the right. Silverdale train station is back in the village.

OPEN: Apr–Oct.

IF IT'S FULL: There are more sea views from Hollins Farm Campsite (01524 701767) in Far Arnside; it's a rough and ready campsite with no showers, just a rickety old loo.

Gibraltar Farm Campsite, Hollins Lane, Silverdale, Lancashire LA5 0AU   t 01524 701736   w www.gibraltarfarm.co.uk

low wray

In recent years, the tranquility of the Lake District has been shattered by a fierce battle over Lake Windermere. On one side, power-boaters and jet-skiers defended their right to whiz around the lake in the name of recreation. On the other side, conservationists pushed for a 10mph speed limit to return the lake to a quieter, safer past.

The boaters reasoned that Windermere was the only remaining lake to allow high-speed fun, leaving 99 per cent of the Lake District free for gentler pursuits. Besides, the local economy benefited enormously from related tourism. The conservationists disagreed. Windermere is a spectacularly beautiful place, the largest lake in England and a significant natural asset. It was argued that jet-skiers belong in Brighton or Blackpool, not here amongst the still waters and soaring skies of Lakeland. And so in 2005, the speed limit was enforced and Windermere fell quiet.

Despite the change, the expected tourist desertion hasn't happened. The lake is easily accessible, has great facilities in the towns of Windermere and Bowness on its eastern shore and there's still plenty to do – on and off the water. In fact, some would say the place is still too busy and noisy, unless you know where to look.

On the quieter western shore of the lake, away from the ice creams and fish & chips of Bowness, sits Low Wray National Trust Campsite. It's a small site with two main areas for camping; one set back from the lake in a clearing surrounded by trees, and another tree-scattered spot right on the shore of Windermere with views across the water to Wansfell Pike and The Fairfield Horseshoe. Without a doubt, the tiny lakeside site is the best place to pitch, despite the £5 surcharge and the longer walk from the car (vehicles must be parked in the designated areas, away from the camping grass).

A night or two camping at this lakeside location is unforgettable. In the early evening, the sunlight dances through the tall trees to light up the barbecue smoke; and if the weather stays with you for a decent sunrise over the lake, it can feel like the most restful place on earth. Genuine peace and quiet – no cars, and certainly no jet skis.

As you would expect from a National Trust site, it's well-organised with good facilities, although it's certainly not the cheapest campsite, especially with the surcharge. You also need to make sure you're fully provisioned as the small campsite shop doesn't open for long, and when it does, there's not much to buy. It's a 10–15 minute drive into Ambleside for your nearest decent shop.

Aside from the great location next to England's largest lake and the possibilities for sailing, kayaking and fishing, the campsite is well-positioned to take in some of the Lake District's 'dry' attractions. There are plenty of opportunities for walking and off-road cycling, with paths leading directly from the campsite. This is also Beatrix Potter country, so a trip here wouldn't be complete without visiting either her home at Hill Top near Sawrey or the Beatrix Potter Gallery in Hawkshead, which houses an exhibition of her original paintings.

Nearer to the campsite is Wray Castle, a large private house and another Beatrix favourite. She stayed here for childhood holidays and loved the place so much that in later life she bought most of the surrounding land with royalties from her books. The castle's gothic revival architecture features imposing fortifications, its battle-strong design slightly at odds in such a peaceful place with no obvious history of conflict. Then again, with the recent speed-limit skirmish, perhaps it is appropriate after all.

THE UPSIDE: Unforgettable lakeside camping – if you can book one of the few spots! Turn up promptly at 1pm when reception opens to get one of the few spots (no advance booking).
THE DOWNSIDE: The midges. Take insect repellent.
THE DAMAGE: Adult £4.50, child £1.50, vehicle £2.50, lakeside premium £5 per tent. No caravans.

THE FACILITIES: Shop, laundry, children's playground, hot showers, disabled facilities, boat launching (no powercraft).
NEAREST DECENT PUB: The Drunken Duck Inn (015394 36347) at Ambleside is one of England's best pubs with an award-winning restaurant and ales brewed on the premises (10 minute drive, 40 minute walk).
IF IT RAINS: There's a small cinema in Ambleside. If it's really chucking it down, you could always try to get a room at the excellent Drunken Duck Inn (16 rooms from £90).
GETTING THERE: From Ambleside, take the A593 to Clappersgate then turn left onto the B5286. Turn left again at the sign for Wray, the site is less than a mile on the left.
OPEN: Easter–Oct.
IF IT'S FULL: Try Great Langdale Campsite (p210) just up the road.

Low Wray National Trust Campsite, Low Wray, near Ambleside, Cumbria LA22 0JA

	t	015394 32810	w	www.lowwraycampsite.org.uk

great langdale

In this most spectacular of areas, where grand views lurk around every corner, it's possible to become blasé and complacent, to grow almost immune to the beauty of these great pyramids of rock and the vast, flat pools of water shimmering with the reflection of blue skies.

If you're feeling all 'laked-out', the perfect tonic has to be an excursion into the serene valley of Great Langdale, where the attraction isn't lake-based, it's the quiet valley countryside dominated by two modest but distinctive peaks: the Langdale Pikes.

Pike O'Stickle (709 metres) and its loftier neighbour Harrison Stickle (736 metres) are Lake District landmarks. Although by no means the tallest in these parts, they're an attractive pair, joined at the shoulder like giant Siamese twins. For many people, their first glimpse of the 'Langdales' comes when approaching Lake Windermere from the east – the peaks rise up majestically in the distance behind the lake, creating a distinctive backdrop and forming part of a classic, picture-perfect Lakeland scene.

To get closer to the Pikes, leave the town of Ambleside to the west and instead of following the traffic on the main road towards Coniston Water, take a right at Skelwith Bridge village to head straight down the Langdale Valley. There are noticeably fewer tourists in this valley as it isn't on the A-list of Lakeland destinations. Just as the twists and turns finish and the road looks as if it might taper off into a narrow footpath, you'll find Great Langdale Campsite. This glorious National Trust site is set in a wooded glen at the head of the valley and consists of several small, grassy camping areas around an undergrowth-shielded beck. Impressive peaks and slopes surround the site on all sides: you really feel like you're in the true heart of the Lake District here.

Great Langdale is a typical National Trust campsite: well-organised, efficiently run, with just the right facilities and set in some of England's finest scenery. After registering at reception and obtaining tags for your tent and car, you have the run of the place to find a suitable pitch. Cars aren't allowed in the camping areas, but none of the pitches is far enough for that to be a problem. The wood-fronted shower blocks contain plenty of facilities in school-style rows of cubicles. There's also a drying room to stash rain-damp walking clothes and boots overnight, a very handy extra.

As you would expect, the walking from here is first-class. A map is available from reception, outlining four easy walks around the valley, each between three and seven miles in length. But despite being tempted by these steady rambles across meadows, woodlands and river banks, many visitors are keen to go for glory and conquer the Langdale Pikes. The start and end point for the ascent is at the New Dungeon Ghyll pub off the main valley road, just a few minutes' walk from the campsite. It's named after Dungeon Ghyll, a deep cleft that dissects the pikes on the slopes above, creating a

100 foot waterfall and a protected area for alpine flowers to flourish in. You'll pass it as you shin up the path on the nine-mile round-trip to the peaks.

It's also possible to walk to Scafell Pike from here and on to another *Cool Camping* site at Wasdale Head (see page 220). Scafell may be the tallest and most brag-worthy peak to conquer in these fells, but the Langdales are just as rewarding. You also get double the fun: two peaks for the price of one. Not a bad day's work, and definitely worth a pint – or two – at the Dungeon.

THE UPSIDE: A truly tranquil treasure in the heart of classic Lake District scenery.

THE DOWNSIDE: No advance bookings taken.

THE DAMAGE: Adults £4.50, children £1.50, cars £2.50, dogs £1. Tents and motorhomes only; no caravans.

THE FACILITIES: Good amenities with unmetered hot showers and rows of toilets and washbasins; washing-up room, drying room, laundry facilities, disabled facilities, kids' playground. An on-site shop sells groceries, maps, guide books, gas refills and other camping accessories.

NEAREST DECENT PUB: There are three good pubs within 10 minutes' walk of the campsite: The Sticklebarn Tavern (015394 37356), The Old Dungeon Ghyll (015394 37272) and The New Dungeon Ghyll (015394 37213). Our favourite is the 'ODG', a legendary Lakeland pub famous for its Walker's Bar, where a roaring fire and a fine selection of ales are perfect for walk-weary hikers. The landlord is quite handy on the violin, so rowdy, impromptu nights of music are common.

IF IT RAINS: It always rains in the Lake District – bring waterproofs!

GETTING THERE: Take the A593 from Ambleside. At Skelwith Bridge, turn right onto the B5343. The campsite is six miles down this road; look out for the sign on the left after the New Dungeon Ghyll Hotel. Using public transport, take the train to Windermere, then the 599 bus to Ambleside, where you can pick up the Langdale Rambler (daily bus service 516; for times call 0870 608 2608; www.traveline.org.uk).

OPEN: All year.

IF IT'S FULL: Other Cool Camping sites within striking distance are Low Wray (p206) and Turner Hall Farm (p214).

Great Langdale National Trust Campsite, Great Langdale, Ambleside, Cumbria LA22 9JU

| | t | 015394 37668 | w | www.langdalecampsite.org.uk |

turner hall farm

If you're looking for a truly remote, wilderness camping experience, you'd find it hard to do much better than Turner Hall Farm in the Lake District's lesser-visited Duddon Valley. The reality is, it's not that far from civilisation, but it feels like the middle of nowhere, given the journey there.

The most spectacular way to arrive at Turner Hall Farm is to drive over the Wrynose Pass, a tortuous zigzag of a road, often single-track, frequently hare-pinned and always threatening to throw your car down the steep sides of the hill with one wrong move. It's an exhilarating drive that matches some of the best Lake District walks, view for view. If you're a nervous driver, take the safer long, winding road via Broughton Mills. Even from here, you have to get out of the car to open and close gates, an action loaded with the symbolism of leaving civilisation behind.

Turner Hall Farm is tucked into the folds of the fells between the mountains of Scafell Pike to the northwest, and the Old Man of Coniston to the southeast. It's a basic campsite for walkers and climbers, the attraction being its location and outlook rather than the facilities – there's no shower or hot water, just toilets and sinks. But the surrounding fells provide an unforgettable backdrop that makes for a fine, inspiring vista. It's a raw, boulder-strewn, long-grassed site, with private corners for sheltered pitching in amongst the crags and drystone walls. Weathered and worn, beaten and torn, the site merges as one into the rugged fell landscape. It's all pretty low-key for a campsite: just turn up, pitch your tent and you might or might not be charged in the morning. There's no reception or shop, but it's a short walk to the pub, and a longer walk to the local post office and general stores. The lack of showers and hot water may be an issue for some, but considering it's a small, little-visited working farm in the middle of nowhere, there's a remarkably clean and functional toilet block, which is very stylish in a country-concrete-chic kind of way.

Campers at Turner Hall Farm are invariably here to walk, with hikes to the lofty peaks of Scafell Pike and The Old Man of Coniston high on the list. These are challenging treks for energetic walkers, but you can warm up with one of the easier walks that criss-cross these fells, taking in lower-altitude pikes, tarns, crags and waterfalls. Popular routes include hiking over the Dunnerdale Fells into the charming, untouched Lickle Valley,

home of the age-old Blacksmiths Arms watering hole, or across Birker Fell and down into Eskdale where a steam railway and the historic, supposedly haunted Muncaster Castle provide some family attractions.

A short walk across the fields from the campsite lies the Walna Scar track, one of the oldest roads in the Lake District. In times gone by, it was used by packhorses weighed down with copper ore from the mines at Coniston, and by carts carrying stone from the nearby quarries. It's long-established as a walker's highway too,

linking the Dunnerdale Fells with the Old Man of Coniston and leading on to the town of Coniston itself. It's now also popular with mountain bikers, happy to endure the tough, bike-carrying uphill sections for the adrenalin-pumping downhills. Off-road vehicles also ply some sections of this track, although erosion intermittently forces the National Trust to ban this activity.

Turner Hall Farm may be as off the beaten track as you can get, but thankfully you don't need a 4 x 4 to get there. Just remember to shut the gates behind you as you leave civilisation.

THE UPSIDE: A glorious wilderness amongst rocky crags and famous fells.

THE DOWNSIDE: Basic facilities, no hot water.

THE DAMAGE: A simple pricing structure: adults £3, children £1, vehicles £1. Tents and motorhomes only, no caravans.

THE FACILITIES: A field, a couple of toilets, washbasins with cold water. No showers. A post office and general stores (01229 716255) with its own small gallery can be found three miles away in Ulpha selling newspapers, groceries and paintings.

NEAREST DECENT PUB: The Newfield Inn (01229 716208; www.newfieldinn.co.uk),

10 minutes' walk down the road in Seathwaite, has real ale, a real fire and hearty food. It's open all day, so if the weather turns treacherous, you can hole up here and try each of the beers one by one. A healthy walk or drive away at Broughton Mills is the Blacksmith's Arms (01229 716824), a classic Lakeland walker's pub, little changed for hundreds of years.

IF IT RAINS: Muncaster Castle (01229 717614; www.muncaster.co.uk) near Ravenglass, is allegedly one of Britain's most haunted castles. You can explore the castle grounds, see owls, buzzards and kites, or – if you dare – stay for an overnight 'Ghost Sit' in the haunted Tapestry Room.

GETTING THERE: From Great Langdale (p210) continue over the high-gradient Wrynose Pass, following signs for Seathwaite. Turner Hall Farm is signposted on the left. The alternative route is via Broughton Mills from the A593. Continue through Seathwaite, and you'll see the campsite signposted on your right.

OPEN: Apr–Oct.

IF IT'S FULL: For a more mainstream, on-the-beaten-track experience in the same area, try Fisherground Campsite (01946 723 349; www.fishergroundcampsite.co.uk) near Beckfoot, to the west.

Turner Hall Farm, Seathwaite, Broughton In Furness, Cumbria LA20 6EE | t | 01229 716420 | f | 01229 716792

wasdale head

England's highest mountains may not be on the scale of the Alps, the Andes or the Himalayas, but they are impressive in their own understated way. They also have the advantage of being readily accessible and in most seasons they can be conquered relatively easily with the help of a pair of decent walking boots, favourable weather and a thermos of hot tea. No need for guides, sherpas or acclimatisation – just as well if you're only here for the weekend.

Several of the country's 'two-thousanders' – mountains with summits in excess of 2,000 feet – are clustered around the northern end of Wast Water in the Lake District, where the National Trust has thoughtfully sited a camping ground at Wasdale Head.

From here, you can lie in a sleeping bag, head poking out of your tent and as the dawn mist clears, you're able to survey the surrounding slopes and plan your ascent on these high fells – Lingmell (800m), Kirk Fell (802m), Great Gable (899m), Sca Fell (964m) and the daddy of them all, Scafell Pike, England's highest mountain at a whopping 977 metres. Alternatively, you might want to reach for the camping stove and kettle, stay snug in your sleeping bag and enjoy this

most vertical of views from your horizontal vantage point. That's one of the great things about Wasdale Head. It's so close to the high fells, you don't need to expend any energy to enjoy them.

Most visitors, however, do come here to get that little bit closer and Wasdale Head is a handy base camp for Scafell Pike, being the starting point for one of the gentler ascents on the rock-strewn summit. For altitude junkies the Pike is a must-do box to tick, but those in the know reckon that better walks can be found on neighbouring Sca Fell and Great Gable which, despite coming up short on altitude, have a wealth of interesting and impressive geology. Good walkers can hike across these fells from other *Cool Camping* sites at Great Langdale (p210) and Syke Farm (p224).

This area is also said to be the birthplace of climbing, and experienced mountaineers will be in their element. Challenging rock-face ascents offer alternative routes to the top if using just your feet doesn't provide enough exhilaration.

Once you've finished getting high on mountain air, Wasdale has other English extremes to see. Not only is it home to England's uppermost mountain, you'll also find England's deepest lake at Wast Water and its smallest church at St Olaf's. They don't do things by halves in Wasdale.

This small pocket of rural Lakeland even lays claim to being the home of the World's Biggest Liar at the local drinking establishment, The Wasdale Inn, although this fact doesn't seem to be as universally accepted as the other, more conventional claims.

Back at base camp there's a small shop for walking maps, friendly advice and blister-shaped plasters, all essential before striking out on a fell walk. Aside from the shop and the tidy wooden shower block nestled under the trees, facilities here are not over-extravagant, but that's in keeping with this wilderness location. Three small fields scattered with mature and planted trees provide plenty of flat grass for pitching, and with cars restricted to the designated parking areas, it's a peaceful site. Definitely a high point on England's campsite circuit.

THE UPSIDE: Top wilderness location for hiking and climbing; great views of the high fells.

THE DOWNSIDE: No prior booking – first come, first served.

THE DAMAGE: Adults £4.50, children £1.50, cars and motorbikes £2, dogs £1. No caravans; no large groups unless by prior arrangement.

THE FACILITIES: Hot showers, flush toilets, disabled facilities, laundry, kids' playground, nature trail; small shop selling basic food and camping accessories.

NEAREST DECENT PUB: The Wasdale Head Inn (019467 26229; www.wasdale.com), half-a-mile to the north, is reputedly home to the biggest liar in the world (take that with a pinch of salt). Hearty, wholesome food is available for less than a tenner.

IF IT RAINS: The Roman port of Ravenglass, the only coastal town within the Lake District National Park, is accessible from here, as is Muncaster Castle (p218).

GETTING THERE: Approaching from the south on the main A595, turn right at Holmrook for Santon Bridge and follow the signs up to Wasdale Head. Approaching from the north, turn left at Gosforth.

OPEN: All year.

IF IT'S FULL: Basic camping facilities are available in a small field adjacent to the Wasdale Head Inn, or for a comfortable stay in a fully-equipped site, check out Church Stile Farm (01946 726252; www.churchstile.com) at the other end of Wast Water lake. A circuitous drive will take you to Turner Hall Farm (p214), Great Langdale (p210) or Syke Farm (p224).

Wasdale Head National Trust Campsite, Wasdale Head, Seascale, Cumbria CA20 1EX

	t	019467 26220	w	www.ntlakescampsites.org.uk

syke farm

Technology hasn't arrived at Syke Farm campsite yet, and it's all the better for it. 'We're not into those computers,' says the friendly proprietor Mrs Kyle as she marches officiously around collecting tent fees. 'We didn't put ourselves on the internet – *someone else has put us there*' she continues in a most distrustful tone.

It's true. Internet users, that wretched and abominable bunch, have been writing glowing reviews about Mrs Kyle's unassuming campsite. And it appears to have caught her off-guard. Whatever next? An entry in *Cool Camping*?

Syke Farm belongs to another age. It's tucked away in a quiet Lake District valley to the southwest of Keswick in the tiny hamlet of Buttermere. It's not just technology that's having trouble making inroads here. Running water is only reluctantly offered as an option with one shower each for men and women. There's no reception or shop – fees are collected promptly at 8am and the only source of provisions is the farmhouse in the village offering eggs and milk. As for entertainment facilities, well there's a dangerous-looking rope-swing hanging from a tree.

That's pretty much it – an unpretentious, no-frills campsite with an unapologetically back-to-basics approach. And that's exactly why this place makes you feel like you've travelled back in time, escaping all the luxury and materialism of modern life, just for a few days.

As you wake to the sounds of sheep bleating in the fields and water bubbling in the beck, it's all a very appealing existence. With about a dozen houses, a small church, two pubs and a campsite, everything in sleepy Buttermere is in about the right proportion. Even the fells and lakes that surround the village and campsite seem to be perfectly proportioned, providing amazing vistas from wherever you choose to pitch your tent. Camp in the lower field by the stream and you'll look up to the slopes of Grasmoor to the north and Red Pike to the south; camp on the higher ground and you'll look down on to cool, calm Crummock Water.

The campsite and hamlet sit on an alluvial plain that divides the lakes of Buttermere and Crummock Water, an area that would itself have been underwater in years past when the two lakes were one. Some time after the last Ice Age, a few thousand years

worth of sediment deposited from a local stream formed the fertile meadows that can be found here today. It's also the only reasonably flat area of land in the valley on which to build a settlement; the steep valley walls have helped to keep the area largely uninhabited. The slopes are so numerous and steep, it was impossible to walk around Buttermere Lake at ground level until the 19th century, when a frustrated walker named George Benson felt compelled to blast a tunnel through the rock. Thanks to his fit of pique, visitors can now enjoy an easy four-mile stroll right around the water's edge.

Numerous more challenging hill walks are also to be had in this area, including a 10-mile circuit that takes in Scale Force, Red Pike, and the famous ridge of Haystacks. The rewards include glimpses of the Scafells as well as a number of high vantage points from which to survey the beauty of Buttermere below.

Spend a few days relaxing in Buttermere, gazing into the bubbling beck, eating too many locally-made ice creams, and you'll begin to understand Mrs Kyle's frustration at being unwittingly put on the internet. After all, if you find yourself in this gloriously beautiful spot away from the world, why would you want to be put anywhere else?

THE UPSIDE: Idyllic countryside setting amongst lakes and mountains.

THE DOWNSIDE: Cars not allowed on site; you have to lug your gear across the pedestrian access bridge.

THE DAMAGE: Adult/child £5/£3 Mar–Apr; £3.50/£1.50 Nov–Feb. Cars and motorcycles free.

THE FACILITIES: Not much in the way of facilities. A couple of showers (50p for six minutes) and toilets are provided in a cold stone hut.

NEAREST DECENT PUB: Take your pick between The Bridge Hotel (017687 70252; www.bridge-hotel.com) and The Fish Hotel (017687 70253; www.fish-hotel.co.uk), both of which are just a few minutes' stroll from the campsite and serve real ales and good food. The Bridge Hotel has a pleasant beer garden by the stream.

IF IT RAINS: It always rains in the Lake District – bring waterproofs!

GETTING THERE: Take the B5289 from Keswick for the stunning drive over Honister Pass to Buttermere village. On approaching the village, turn left after the church to get to the car park and Syke Farm.

OPEN: All year. Come during the off-season for extra tranquillity.

IF IT'S FULL: Wasdale Head campsite (p220) is just south of here, but there are some pretty big mountains in the way, so it's a long drive or a strenuous walk.

Syke Farm Camping Ground, Buttermere, Cumbria CA13 9XA   t   017687 70222

side farm

Side Farm, on the eastern side of the Lake District, might just be one of the most scenically situated campsites on the planet, sandwiched as it is between the steep slopes of Place Fell to the rear and the sylvan shores of Ullswater at its front. The view across the lake to the Helvellyn Fells is one of the most compelling and beautiful sights in England, and to be able to simply open the tent every morning onto this stunning scene is reason enough to stay awhile at Side Farm.

For many, just to sit by the tent with a good book, soaking up the magnificence of the situation, may be sufficient – possibly wandering down to the foot of the site and the shores of Ullswater for a change of perspective. Others arrive with canoes, spending their time paddling the length and breadth of Ullswater, the second largest but most enchanting of the region's lakes. The lake has a rigidly enforced 10mph speed limit, making this a very safe and well-suited environment for the less hectic forms of waterborne craft.

But if the boating opportunities are superb, and they are, the amazing variety of places to explore on foot from Side Farm is nothing short of astounding. The site lies immediately adjacent to the lakeside path from Howtown to Patterdale, described by Wainwright, the legendary fell walker and guidebook writer, as 'the most beautiful and rewarding in Lakeland'. This is probably the first place to direct your energies, and the most interesting way of completing the walk is said to be by boarding one of the old Ullswater steamers at Glenridding, sailing to Howtown, then strolling back to the site. This is undoubtedly a great day out, with the sailing out and walking back making quite an appealing kind of expedition. Unfortunately, at weekends or in high summer, most of humanity seems to find this an enticing idea. This may be a slight exaggeration, but if you like wild and beautiful places to yourself then choose your time or season carefully. The lakeside path back from Howtown does encounter a few minor ups and downs, but if something more adventurous is on your prescription then walking over Place Fell to Sandwick and using the lakeside path back makes for a more rounded day, whilst the stroll along Boredale to meet up with the Howton-Patterdale path (after an initial fairly steep climb to Boredale Hause) is another great walk from Side Farm.

In the end, however, after staring at the rocky giants across the lake for a few days, the mind will inevitably start to wander up the slopes of Helvellyn – quickly followed by the feet. There are several excellent routes up this most famous of fells from the campsite (enough to keep you busy for a full week on this monster alone) but the one which everybody should do at least once is the dance across the top of Striding Edge. Yes it's popular, and yes it can get scary when the wind is howling around the rocky crest, and yes, the weather can change from summer to winter in an instant, but this is one of the most attention-grabbing and exhilarating walks in England.

The site itself has flat pitching and adequate facilities including toilets and showers, but luxurious they are not and can be somewhat overwhelmed when the site is full. But bring a pair of walking boots, or a canoe, and the idyllic location will more than compensate for any minor niggles.

THE UPSIDE: Perhaps the most scenically placed campsite in England with an unbeatable selection of walks.

THE DOWNSIDE: Too many people know about the upside.

THE DAMAGE: Adults £4.50, children £3, cars £2. Tents and small motorhomes only; no caravans.

THE FACILITIES: Reasonable amenities with toilets, showers and laundry facilities.

NEAREST DECENT PUB: The White Lion Inn (01768 482214) at Patterdale, 15 minutes' walk from the campsite, has a traditional appeal, dependable bar food and tasty home-made soup.

IF IT RAINS: A variety of lake cruises are offered by Ullswater Steamers (01768 482229; www.ullswater-steamers.co.uk), or a cinema and a national Mountaineering Exhibition can be found at Rheged (01768 868000; www.rheged.com).

GETTING THERE: From Junction 40 of the M6 take the A66 west, then the A592 along the shore of Ullswater through Glenridding. One mile beyond Glenridding centre, turn left into a track to Side Farm – just after the church on the right.

OPEN: Easter–Oct.

IF IT'S FULL: Other good camping sites nearby include Sykeside Camping Park (01768 482239; www.sykeside.co.uk) at Brotherswater and Gillside Farm Campsite (01768 482346) at Glenridding.

Side Farm Campsite, Patterdale, Penrith, Cumbria CA11 0NP | t | 01768 482337

hadrian's wall

In AD122, Northumberland represented the farthest reaches of the Roman Empire under Emperor Hadrian. These were turbulent times: everyone wanted to take a pop at Rome's dominance and to try and grab a slice of land when the administrators weren't looking. The Picts, the wild tribes of Caledonia in today's Scotland, were particularly troublesome. So Hadrian decided to consolidate and protect his empire by building a wall around it. Workers began constructing a frontier to help guard the land of the Britons from the land of the Picts and they built a wall 73 miles long and five metres high, stretching from the Tyne to the Solway Firth.

The historical significance of this wall has been recognised by UNESCO, who list it as a World Heritage Site. It actually forms part of a much larger frontier known as the 'Roman Limes' that marked the edge of the Roman Empire not only in England, but all around its circumference in Germany, Austria, Hungary, Slovakia, Croatia and Morocco. To recognise that fact, it's officially named the 'Frontiers of the Roman Empire World Heritage Site' and incorporates the German frontier wall between the Rhine and Danube rivers as well as Hadrian's Wall; two sections of an incredibly ambitious trans-national border.

The years have weathered Hadrian's Wall, but the ruins of this historic structure remain impressive and atmospheric. In some sections, up to a metre of wall are intact, following the contours of the land up and down rounded hills, stretching away into the distance of this barren, inhospitable landscape. It's easy to imagine how the soldiers posted here must have felt, keeping watch at the very outpost of the civilised world – the comfort and culture of Londinium must have felt an awful long way away.

The military barracks housed in 'milecastles' along the wall have long-since disappeared, but it's still possible to camp near the wall and soak up the wild, rugged atmosphere that surrounds this great line of history. In a quiet country road, just a mile or so from one of the most dramatic sections of the wall, Hadrian's Wall Campsite offers a small, secluded slice of border country, where visitors huddle together like a contubernium camp of Roman soldiers.

There are four main levels to the terraced site, named after outposts of the British – rather than the Roman – Empire.

Above Base Camp you have Annapurna, then K2 with Everest at the top. The altitudes here aren't nearly as great as the names might suggest, but if you're in any doubt, there's an overflow meadow on a lower slope, across the road from the main site. There's more space to spread out there and it's quieter, especially during the main summer months, although you have to walk back to the main site to use the facilities. From all these camping areas, you can look out across the shallow hills of Northumberland. You might even be able to glimpse the wall in the distance; the nearest section is hidden behind the hills.

The campsite is well-located for walks along Hadrian's Wall Path, an 84-mile National Trail that shadows the line of the wall. Campsite owners Graham and Patricia will even arrange transport to or from your starting or finishing points, leaving you to enjoy your walk and the wall.

The wall is supposedly the biggest feat of engineering ever undertaken by the Roman Empire. If Hadrian had known he was actually commissioning one of England's longest tourist attractions rather than a workable defence, it might never have been built.

THE UPSIDE: A beautiful countryside campsite near Hadrian's Wall.

THE DOWNSIDE: It's a small site, so pitches can be a bit close together. Only two showers each for males and females.

THE DAMAGE: Backpacker £6, tent and car £8 plus £1 per person, motorhome £8, caravan/trailer tent £10.

THE FACILITIES: Good amenities in a brightly-painted portacabin including hot showers, hair dryers, disabled facilities, a campers' fridge/freezer; the washing machine, tumble dryer, eggs and tinned groceries are subject to an 'honesty box' system. Order the night before for a

Full English Breakfast (£5); barbecue meat packs also available.

NEAREST DECENT PUB: The stone-built Milecastle Inn (01434 321372), a mile to the west, has everything an age-old country pub could want including wooden beams covered in nick-nacks, an open fire and a resident ghost. It also has the benefit of 'wall' views from the beer garden.

IF IT RAINS: The Housesteads Roman Fort and Museum (01434 344363; www.english-heritage.org.uk), the best-preserved Roman fort in Britain, is just down the road; the market town of Haltwhistle, reputed to be the geographical centre of England, is three miles west of the campsite.

GETTING THERE: The campsite is located just east of Haltwhistle. From the B6318 Military Road, take the turning to Melkridge. The site is just 300 metres on the left. From the A69, one mile east of Haltwhistle, there's a staggered crossroads at Melkridge village. Take the turning opposite the village, due north, and continue for two miles.

OPEN: All year.

IF IT'S FULL: Kielder Water, a huge reservoir near the Scottish border, is about 15 miles to the north of here. Kielder Camping site (01434 250291) is a remote and peaceful location from which to explore the waters.

Hadrian's Wall Campsite, Melkridge Tilery, nr Haltwhistle, Northumberland NE49 9PG

| t | 01434 320495 | w | www.romanwallcamping.co.uk |

beadnell bay

There is something strange and ever-so-slightly out of kilter about the north Northumberland coast which is much easier to sense in the air, or feel under your feet, than put your finger on by mere expression. It's almost as if time is travelling on a different plane – that something of the past is constantly reaching forwards through invisible chasms in the time layers. Or perhaps the present is reaching back. It may just be that this remote coastal strip remains as it has been for hundreds of years, and that the only real signs of development are a collection of amazing fortresses built nearly a thousand years ago.

Just in case you aren't sure whereabouts in England this unchanging oasis of tranquillity and beauty lies, it's in the far northeastern corner of the country, very nearly in Scotland. At the moment it's in England, but you never know around here.

Beadnell Bay Campsite, situated next to the sea at Beadnell Bay, is about two miles south of Seahouses – surely the smallest seaside resort in the world. Small it may very well be, but Seahouses boasts a couple of pubs, a couple of chippies and a working fishing harbour, with boats running out to visit the famous Farne Islands – home of birds, but nothing (nor anybody) else. The village of Beadnell itself even has a chip shop and a pub to sustain the active camping life, so what more can you ask for?

The site would be best described as unremarkable in itself, with a flat featureless field presenting nothing in the way of shelter to soften the occasionally wicked east wind from pummelling your tent. Facilities too are fairly average, but there is everything you need in the ablutional department to keep visitors from becoming social outcasts. However, all this is unimportant really, for nobody comes here to sit and ponder how glamorous the toilet block is, or isn't. To come here is to fall under the spell of the empty coastline, and the history still trembling through the air.

What you will definitely need at Beadnell Bay is your bike, for these quiet, level back roads all along the coast are perfect for velocopedic exploration. The first place to explore is the coast road through Seahouses to Bamburgh. Pedalling out of Seahouses will give you a first ethereal glimpse of Bamburgh Castle – miles away, piercing the heavens, and apparently floating on sand.

As the miles disappear under your wheels this hazy mirage gradually solidifies into an elegant but enormous red edifice, impressive and noble in the soft Northumberland sun.

Further north is the Holy Island of Lindisfarne, cut off at high tide, and where, if there really is a time leak occurring hereabouts, the epicentre will surely be found in the ruined priory, or looking out from the harbour scanning the coast from Lindisfarne Castle southwards, to where Bamburgh mysteriously stands.

Despite all this beauty and excitement, the real thrill of this coast is to walk south from the campsite along the sands, past Beadnell Bay, Newton Haven and the empty, exotic-looking Embleton Bay, to take in the dramatic views of Dunstanburgh Castle. Although you probably will be drawn towards the atmospheric ruins, there's no need to get any closer to confirm that something is indeed going on in the ether, and to feel a deep and magnetic attraction to this deserted landscape and seascape.

THE UPSIDE: A stunning stretch of deserted coastline.

THE DOWNSIDE: No direct views from the site; a minor road runs adjacent to the campsite.

THE DAMAGE: Adults £4–£6.30, children £2, non-members additional £5.40 per night pitch fee; tents and motorhomes only, no caravans.

THE FACILITIES: Decent facilities with toilets, unmetered showers and washing-up sinks; gas refills sold at reception.

NEAREST DECENT PUB: If you're desperate, The Craster Arms (01665 720272) is a mere five minutes' walk away in Beadnell, but a more worthwhile journey is to The Ship Inn (01665 576262) at Low Newton-by-the-Sea, a lovely, well-managed pub with a menu rich in local seafood.

IF IT RAINS: If you've done all the castles including Bamburgh (01668 214515; www.bamburghcastle.com), Alnwick (01665 510777; www.alnwickcastle.com) and Dunstanburgh (01665 576231;

www.english-heritage.org.uk), then see what's on at the Alnwick Playhouse (01665 510785; www.alnwickplayhouse.co.uk).

GETTING THERE: From the A1, five miles north of Alnwick, take the B6347 east then the B1340 to Beadnell. The site is on the left after a bend to the north of Beadnell.

OPEN: Apr–Oct.

IF IT'S FULL: The Camping and Caravanning Club also have a good site six miles south at Dunstan Hill (01665 576310).

Beadnell Bay Campsite, Beadnell, Chathill, Northumberland NE67 5BX

| t | 01665 720586 | w | www.campingandcaravanningclub.co.uk |

festival fun

Peace. Love. And corporate sponsorship. The very nature of the summer festival has changed beyond recognition since the heady days of sixties psychedelia, when a folk band, a fistful of pot and a few friends in a field was deemed enough. Today's festivals have grown in sophistication, size and stature to become a major UK industry, and as big-brand festivals continue to move into mainstream culture, more people are discovering the delights of a weekend under canvas.

The number and diversity of festivals has also grown, with festivals to suit every mood or musical taste. But there are a small number of regular festivals that stand head and shoulders above the others, confidently crowd-surfing across the top of the second-rate festivals moshing it out below.

The undisputed daddy of English festivals is Glastonbury, the original and, many would argue, still the best. It all started way back in 1970 when Somerset farmer Michael Eavis organised the 'Pilton Pop Festival' on his Glastonbury farm. Around 1,500 groovy young things turned up to see Marc Bolan and T Rex headline at a cost of just £1 each – including free milk from the farm. Since then, the festival has grown into something of an institution, with a 150,000-strong crowd

invading this small pocket of rural England to listen to some of the biggest – and smallest – names in music. Officially known as the Glastonbury Festival for Contemporary Performing Arts, it's now the largest greenfield music and performing arts event in the world, generating thousands of pounds for charities and worthy causes.

As well as the music, everyone remembers Glastonbury for the inevitable rain, muddy camping and tents floating in knee-high water. Stoic campers have come to accept it as part of the ritual and fun of the event, the Glastonbury rite of passage. You haven't truly been to a festival – haven't truly camped – until you've danced in the mud in a field at Glastonbury.

If Glastonbury is the reliable, middle-aged festival that's been around the block and could tell you some stories by the fire, then Bestival, on the Isle of Wight, is the cheeky young upstart who chooses to ignore the established order and is intent on doing his own thing. Bestival burst onto the scene in 2004, brainchild of DJ and Isle of Wight local boy Rob Da Bank. If the philosophy of Bestival could be summarised into one neat sentence, it would be a desire to have as much fun as can be reasonably squeezed into a long September weekend. This fresh attitude manifests itself in innovative attractions like a sauna-yurt for maximum relaxation, a non-denominational 45-foot inflatable church for prayers and meditation and the world's largest-ever fancy dress party. At Bestival, the cakes at the Women's Institute Tea Tent are held in as high acclaim as the headlining bands.

This 'not-taking-itself-too-seriously' approach has proved a big hit with fun-loving festival goers and Bestival's reputation as the definitive end-of-summer hurrah is growing faster than a fake moustache.

If jumping around in the mud or dressing up as a Mexican is just too much excitement for you, then The Big Chill is probably more your thing. It's an altogether more civilised experience and really very grown-up indeed.

The name says it all – this isn't frantic raving, all-night pill-frenzies and rushing from stage to stage. It's massage tents, sushi, organic juice bars and croquet on the lawn. It's decent, laid-back tunes and eclectic musical surprises in a Brit-flick beautiful setting with many people happily tucked up in their tents by 2am. This might sound more Horlicks than hedonist, and it is – you'll see more people pushing prams than drugs. But that doesn't detract from the enjoyment or the vibe. It's like a small gathering of like-minded friends on a camping weekend, where the music is almost incidental. The Big Chill has grown in size over the years, but thankfully the unique and appealing garden-party vibe has remained intact.

The criticism that can be levelled at most festivals these days is that they're all too corporate and conformist, that there's none of the idealistic hippy-vibe of years gone by. And that's where The Big Green Gathering comes in, an environmentally-friendly event near Glastonbury that prides itself on being the first exclusively solar- and wind-powered festival. The small-scale event is organised by a cooperative to promote health, sustainability and environmental awareness – unusually for a festival, unhealthy activities are positively discouraged with no alcohol for sale on the site. With limited electricity, the vibe here, especially after dark, is very medieval. It feels like a cross between a 10th-century market and a modern-day gathering of protesters disputing the building of a road through Twyford Down.

The simplistic ideals of The Big Green Gathering are a refreshing tonic to most corporate-sponsored events, but whatever your particular brand of summer festival, surely it's all just an excuse to go camping without the 'no noise after 11pm' rule.

festival details

WHAT: **Glastonbury Festival**
WHERE: Glastonbury, Somerset
WHEN: A weekend around the summer solstice in June
WHO: Everyone and anyone
WHY: To say you've been
WWW: www.glastonburyfestivals.co.uk
WHAT TO BRING: A sturdy tent, wellies, a change of clothes

WHAT: **The Big Chill**
WHERE: Various locations, recently at Eastnor Castle in Herefordshire
WHEN: Various dates, usually early August
WHO: Ex-clubbers; young families; thirty-somethings with luxury tents
WHY: Because Glastonbury's just too big, noisy and soulless these days, don't you agree?
WWW: www.bigchill.net
WHAT TO BRING: Beanbags, comfy seats, organic muesli

WHAT: **The Big Green Gathering**
WHERE: Location varies, but recently in the Mendip Hills near Cheddar in Somerset
WHEN: Early August
WHO: Environmentalists, travellers, hippies, green-thinkers
WHY: Because the planet needs us, man
WWW: www.big-green-gathering.com
WHAT TO BRING: Dreadlocks, glowsticks, a solar-powered shower

WHAT: **Bestival**
WHERE: Newport, Isle of Wight
WHEN: Early September
WHO: Happy, friendly twenty-somethings; everyone that likes fun
WHY: Because summer deserves to be sent off with a bang
WWW: www.bestival.net
WHAT TO BRING: Fancy dress outfit

top tips

First timer? Take a minute to read our top tips. Most of it's just common sense, but you never know what you don't know.

WATCH THE WEATHER

The weather can mean the difference between a great trip and an awful trip. Keep an eye on the forecast, and if it's bad, consider postponing. Better to be a proud fair-weather camper than a miserable, moaning wet one.

AVOID SCHOOL HOLIDAYS

Don't go during busy periods if you can help it. Your experience and enjoyment will be greatly enhanced. If you can only go during school holidays, try to opt for quieter sites off the beaten track.

BE PREPARED

More than just a motto! Make sure you've thought through everything you need to take. If it's your first time, make a thorough checklist before you go.

CHOOSE A GOOD SITE

Well obviously, it should be a campsite recommended by *Cool Camping*. But within the site, choose exactly where you pitch your tent carefully. Opt for level ground, ideally with some shade too – tents get very hot in direct sunshine. But make sure your level ground isn't at the bottom of a big dip that will fill with water if it rains. Also, try and pick a place that's near enough to the amenities to be handy, but far enough to be free from associated noise and traffic.

LEAVE NO TRACE

Dispose of your rubbish in the right place, only light fires in designated areas, respect the countryside and don't hassle or feed the wildlife. Lecture over!

happy campers?

The campsites featured in this book are a personal selection chosen by the *Cool Camping* team. None of the campsites has paid a fee for inclusion, nor was one requested, so you can be sure of an objective choice of sites and honest descriptions.

We have visited hundreds of campsites across England to find these 40, and we hope you like them as much as we do. However, it hasn't been possible to visit every single campsite. So if you know of a special campsite that you think should be included, we'd like to hear about it.

Send us an email telling us the name and location of the campsite, some contact details and why it's special. We'll credit all useful contributions in the next edition of *Cool Camping* and the best emails will receive a complimentary copy. Feel free to tell us about campsites in Wales and Scotland as well as England. Just use the relevant email details below. Thanks, and enjoy our great countryside. See you out there!

england@coolcamping.co.uk
wales@coolcamping.co.uk
scotland@coolcamping.co.uk

Design and artwork: Andrew Davis
www.andrewjamesdavis.com
andrew@andrewjamesdavis.com

Research: Jonathan Knight,
Shellani Gupta & Andy Stothert
Editor: Claire Wedderburn-Maxwell
Proofreaders: Shellani Gupta
& Rachel Simmonds
Production Manager: Scott Criddle
Production Assistant: Caren Kauffmann
PR: Carol Farley, Farley Partnership

Published by:
Punk Publishing,
26 York Street,
London W1U 6PZ

Distributed by:
Portfolio Books,
Unit 5,
Perivale Industrial Park,
Perivale, Middlesex UB6 7RL

All photographs © Jonathan Knight
with the exception of the following,
all reproduced by kind permission:

View of Side Farm (front cover, p12 & p230),
Spiers House campsite (p190), Staithes
village (p193), Newtondale, North Yorks
(p193), walker above Side Farm (p233),
Bamburgh beach and castle (p240 & 245),
Beadnell Bay campsite (p245) all © Andy
Stothert (lakelandscapes.co.uk).

Pedn Vounder Beach and Logan Rock (p26)
© Simon Cook (cornish-images.com); Aerial
view of Porthcurno beach (p28/29)
© Bob Croxford/Atmosphere Image Library
(www.atmosphere.co.uk); Minack Theatre
(p31) © Minack Theatre, Porthcurno; view at
dusk from Bay View Farm (p59) © Mel Gigg;
Lundy Island campsite (p76), aerial view of
Lundy (p76), St Helena's Church (p79) and
The Old Light (p76) all © Lundy Island;
Symond's Yat (p97), Bracelands campsite
(p98), Bilbins Suspension Bridge (p98),
Beech trees in Forest of Dean (p101),
Beech trees and bluebells (p101), Cathedral
Sculpture (p102), family playing on
Melissa's Swing sculpture (p103) all
© Isobel Cameron/Forestry Commission;
forest walk (p100), trees in fog (p101),
woodland shadows (p101) all © Forestry
Commission; Corfe Castle in mist
(p116/117) © Ken Ayres
(www.viewscenes.co.uk); aerial view of The
Needles, Isle of Wight (p128)
© Isle of Wight Tourism; windsurfer (p131)
© John Carter Photography/Isle of Wight
Tourism; The Warren campsite (p149),
Beadnell Bay campsite (p240) both
© The Camping and Caravanning Club; all
photographs of Clippesby Hall (p154–162)
© Paul Studd/Clippesby Hall; Longnor
Wood flower meadow (p175), Longnor Wood
flower detail (p175) both © Longnor Wood;
busy campsite (p180), campers at breakfast
(p183) both © Upper Booth Farm; trees in
Hamsterley Forest, North Yorks Moors
(p190) © Forest Life Picture Library/
Forestry Commission; happy festival girl
(p246) © Sophie Laslett/The Big Chill;
festival bed (p250) © Kelvin Webb/The Big
Chill; fancy dress girls (p249), fancy dress
crowd (p249), festival parasol (p250),
Rob and Campervan (p251) all
© Bestival; Glastonbury Pyramid Stage
(p246 & p250), Glastonbury tents
underwater (p249), Glastonbury muddy
revellers (p249), 'Love' car at The Big Green
Gathering (p250), old caravan at Big Green
Gathering (p251), happy, muddy campers
(p255) all © Jason Bryant.

The publishers and authors have done
their best to ensure the accuracy of all
information in *Cool Camping: England*,
however, they can accept no responsibility
for any injury, loss, or inconvenience
sustained by anyone as a result of
information or advice contained in
this book.